"This fascinating study shows how Jesus's parables, such as prodigal son, are not only powerful stories but also treasure tro gestive allusions to the Old Testament. Although short, this book wealth of wisdom to give today's readers insight into Luke's parable helping them understand more of what it means to be a disciple A gripping and illuminating read!"

Simon Gathercole, Professor of New Testament and Early
Christianity, University of Cambridge

"In this thought-provoking and compelling book, Peter J. Williams digs under the topsoil of the parables attributed to Jesus in the Gospels and helps us see both how expertly these stories integrate Old Testament allusions and how all the evidence points back to Jesus of Nazareth himself as their Creator."

Rebecca McLaughlin, author, *Confronting Jesus: 9 Encounters with
the Hero of the Gospels*

"Jesus's parable of the prodigal son is a masterpiece in the history of storytelling. Not only does it make a powerful impact on people of all cultures, it is intricately and poetically composed and rife with allusions to Old Testament narratives, especially about Jacob and Esau. Other parables demonstrate these same characteristics. Whoever composed them deserved to be called a genius, and Jesus (rather than one of his followers) is the best candidate for that individual. *The Surprising Genius of Jesus*, though a little book, is chock-full of observations about Jesus's teaching that should make readers admire him even more than they may already do."

Craig L. Blomberg, Distinguished Professor Emeritus of New
Testament, Denver Seminary

"A study at once scholarly and gripping of a man who was—whatever else you may believe him to have been—clearly the most brilliant and influential short-story teller of all time."

Tom Holland, Presenter, *Making History*; author, *Dominion: How
the Christian Revolution Remade the World*

"A fascinating, provocative, and important book that presents a compelling and persuasive case."

Justin Meggitt, Senior Lecturer in the Study of Religion and Fellow of Wolfson College, University of Cambridge

"Whoever came up with the parable of the prodigal son must have had a forensic knowledge and deep understanding of the Old Testament, as well as an unrivaled ability to connect with simple people and confound and outwit the superintelligent. The one who said those words knew what he was doing—his intentions and claims are made very clear to whoever will take them seriously. Peter J. Williams's excellent and very readable book is unique in considering the shocking wisdom of Jesus's teaching, and it presents Jesus as accessible to everyone yet wise enough to confound even the intellectuals."

Tim Farron, Member of Parliament, United Kingdom

The Surprising Genius of Jesus

The Surprising Genius of Jesus

What the Gospels Reveal about the Greatest Teacher

Peter J. Williams

CROSSWAY®

WHEATON, ILLINOIS

The Surprising Genius of Jesus: What the Gospels Reveal about the Greatest Teacher
Copyright © 2023 by Peter J. Williams
Published by Crossway
        1300 Crescent Street
        Wheaton, Illinois 60187

Figure 1, in chapter 2, an image of manuscript Or. 4445, folio 23v, from the Pentateuch, is used by permission of the British Library. © British Library Board. All rights reserved / Bridgeman Images.

Cover design: Micah Lanier

Cover image: © British Library Board (Or. 4445), Shutterstock, Unsplash

First printing 2023

Printed in the United States of America

Unless otherwise indicated, Scripture quotations are the author's own translation or are lightly adapted from the ESV.

Scripture quotations marked ESV are from the ESV® Bible (The Holy Bible, English Standard Version®), copyright © 2001 by Crossway, a publishing ministry of Good News Publishers. Used by permission. All rights reserved. The ESV text may not be quoted in any publication made available to the public by a Creative Commons license. The ESV may not be translated into any other language.

All emphases in Scripture quotations have been added by the author.

Trade paperback ISBN: 978-1-4335-8836-5
ePub ISBN: 978-1-4335-8839-6
PDF ISBN: 978-1-4335-8837-2

Library of Congress Cataloging-in-Publication Data

Names: Williams, Peter J., 1970– author.
Title: The surprising genius of Jesus : what the gospels reveal about the greatest teacher / Peter Williams.
Description: Wheaton, Illinois : Crossway, 2023. | Includes bibliographical references and index.
Identifiers: LCCN 2022041818 (print) | LCCN 2022041819 (ebook) | ISBN 9781433588365 (trade paperback) | ISBN 9781433588372 (pdf) | ISBN 9781433588396 (epub)
Subjects: LCSH: Bible. Luke XV, 11–32—Criticism, interpretation, etc. | Prodigal son (Parable)
Classification: LCC BT378.P8 W545 2023 (print) | LCC BT378.P8 (ebook) | DDC 226.8/06—dc23 /eng/20230505
LC record available at https://lccn.loc.gov/2022041818
LC ebook record available at https://lccn.loc.gov/2022041819

Crossway is a publishing ministry of Good News Publishers.

BP   32   31   30   29   28   27   26   25   24   23
15   14   13   12   11   10   9   8   7   6   5   4   3   2   1

For Tim and Fiona

Contents

Preface

THIS IS A BOOK ABOUT the cleverness of Jesus. It argues both that clever teaching is attributed to Jesus and that Jesus actually said those clever things. My hope is that readers who are Christians come away with a renewed awe at the depth of Jesus's words and that any who are not Christians see Jesus's genius and recognize that he must be more than merely an extraordinarily gifted teacher. Much of this book is about one passage—Luke 15:11–32—and about how it is a brilliant story, reflecting the mind of a genius. For an application of the meaning of that text for today, I cannot recommend highly enough Timothy Keller, *The Prodigal God: Recovering the Heart of the Christian Faith* (New York: Dutton, 2008).

I am grateful to the trustees and staff of Tyndale House, Cambridge, for giving me the time to write this book and to many friends who were willing to read this book in a rough draft and offer suggestions for improvement. These readers include Esther Atsen, James Bejon, Keith Bintley, Ezra Brainard, Dr. John Hayward, Miriam Hulley, Dr. Dirk Jongkind, Zachary Klein, Demsin Lachin, David Laing, Dr. Stephen Lloyd, Stephen McCausland,

Greg and Jennifer Mayer, Dr. Kaspars Ozoliņš, Toby Payne, Lily Rivers, Cristo Rodriguez, Kathryn Williams (my better half), Tim Williams (a lovely older brother), and Jordan Worley.

Biblical quotations from the English Standard Version are marked ESV. Other biblical quotations are my own translations or are lightly adapted from the ESV.

Introduction

I discovered that I had been unconsciously
trained to admire everything about Jesus
except his intellectual astuteness.

KENNETH BAILEY
Finding the Lost

OVER THE YEARS thousands of people have been described as geniuses.[1] Aristotle (384–322 BC), Leonardo da Vinci (1452–1519),
Wolfgang Amadeus Mozart (1756–1791), and Albert Einstein
(1879–1955) are among the more famous ones. But the term *genius* is almost never applied to Jesus of Nazareth.[2] Probably about
two billion Christians would claim to follow his teachings, which
is more than follow the teachings of any other person in history.
But most of the Christians I mix with would be more likely to

---

1   As of March 2022, Amazon has over four thousand books in the category of biographies
    that include the word *genius* in their title.
2   An exception is the recent motivational book by Erwin Raphael McManus, *The Genius
    of Jesus: The Man Who Changed Everything* (New York: Convergent, 2021).

see Jesus's intelligence as a necessary corollary of his divine nature than to point to specific things he said as examples of remarkable intellect. When Jesus is viewed as a teacher, as Christian philosopher Dallas Willard wryly comments, "Frankly, he is not taken to be a person of much ability."[3]

One reason others are seen as geniuses but Jesus is not could be what they have left behind. Aristotle left books of philosophy and analysis; da Vinci, inventions and exquisite paintings; Mozart, sublime music; Einstein, theories that are foundational for modern physics. And Jesus? He never wrote a book. But could we say that he left Christianity behind? The problem is that its art, history, institutions, philosophy, and so on are often regarded as a *response* to Jesus, not something he himself thought up. At least we can agree that many things under the label of Christianity have nothing at all to do with the teachings of Jesus.

This book argues that Jesus should be considered a genius, not merely because a vast number of people today claim to follow him but also because of the cleverness and wisdom of his teaching. The teaching attributed to him combines impressive factual knowledge with even more impressive depth of insight, coherence, and simplicity. He was literally able to teach two groups with very different knowledge levels simultaneously. Evidence for Jesus's teaching is found in the four earliest records of Jesus, the four Gospels: Matthew, Mark, Luke, and John. It is well worth investing the nine hours or so it takes to read all four of them once. In fact, speaking from experience, I can say that it is rewarding to study them for an entire lifetime. If you have doubts about whether they can be

---

3   Dallas Willard, *The Divine Conspiracy: Rediscovering Our Hidden Life in God* (London: William Collins, 1998), 1.

taken as serious historical sources, I invite you to read my short book *Can We Trust the Gospels?*[4]

To follow my argument here, you do not need to believe that Jesus said all the things credited to him in the Gospels. All you need to believe is that the sayings attributed to Jesus come from within living memory of him, remembering that even leading skeptical scholars date the Gospels to the first century.[5] Jesus Christ was executed while Pontius Pilate was the Roman governor of Judea (AD 26–36),[6] and if the Gospels were all written by AD 100 (personally, I think they were much earlier), the gap between Jesus and the Gospels is both short enough for them to be thoroughly reliable and long enough for them to be thoroughly unreliable. The length of time alone does not therefore tell us about the degree of their reliability. Only an examination of the Gospels themselves can answer this question.

In the pages that follow, I intend both to show the genius of the words attributed to Jesus in the Gospels and to explore the best explanation for where these clever ideas originated. Was Jesus a rather ordinary teacher with brilliant students who selflessly

4 Peter J. Williams, *Can We Trust the Gospels?* (Wheaton, IL: Crossway, 2018).

5 Leading scholar and skeptic Bart D. Ehrman says, "Most historians think that Mark was the first of our Gospels to be written, sometime between the mid 60s to early 70s. Matthew and Luke were probably produced some ten or fifteen years later, perhaps around 80 to 85. John was written perhaps ten years after that, in 90 or 95." Ehrman, *The New Testament: A Historical Introduction to the Early Christian Writings*, 2nd ed. (Oxford: Oxford University Press, 2000), 43.

6 See Roman historian Tacitus, *Annals* 15.44, for evidence that Christ's execution occurred while Pilate was governor of Judea. Josephus, *Jewish Antiquities* 18.89, gives Pilate's tenure in Judea as ten years and his departure shortly before Tiberius died on March 16, AD 37. Thus, whereas Pilate may have governed until the beginning of AD 37, since Jesus was executed at Passover time, which fell in late March or April, the crucifixion must have taken place between AD 26 and AD 36.

credited him with their great ideas?[7] Or was Jesus a very smart teacher with, coincidentally, smart disciples, and therefore the credit should be shared? Or was Jesus himself the genius, and to the extent that his disciples showed themselves intelligent, they were simply reflecting the greatness of their teacher?

I find the last explanation best, and I want to consider as my central evidence of Jesus's genius the longest story attributed to him, commonly known as the parable of the prodigal son (Luke 15:11–32). As we will see, despite its name, the story involving the prodigal son is about *two* sons, not one. It is set after two related stories about a lost sheep and a lost coin. By focusing on one story, I do not want to suggest that this is the only example of Jesus's genius—or even the most important one. His creativity and wisdom can be seen in all his teaching, closely examined. But to keep this book short, we examine just one major story in depth while considering other stories more briefly. We will be analyzing only Jesus's stories and will not even touch on his sermons or dialogues.

The first chapter looks at the cleverness on the surface of the longest story attributed to Jesus. The second examines the cleverness of this story through the way it echoes multiple Old Testament stories. The third investigates other stories attributed to Jesus and shows that they too contain the same sort of use of the Old Testament. The fourth highlights reasons for thinking that the cleverness of all the stories in Luke 15–16 must go back to Jesus himself. The final chapter connects what we have learned with Jesus's mission as a whole and considers how this challenges us all.

7 Jesus was early seen as a philosopher. See Jonathan T. Pennington, *Jesus the Great Philosopher: Rediscovering the Wisdom Needed for the Good Life* (Grand Rapids, MI: Brazos, 2020), 3–8.

1

A Brilliant Story

WE BEGIN OUR TREASURE HUNT by collecting a few of the many nuggets of gold on the uppermost surface of the longest story attributed to Jesus, found in Luke 15:11–32. It is just 388 words long in the Greek original,[1] but despite its brevity, it combines beguiling simplicity on the surface with several coherent layers of deeper meaning for a student of the Old Testament.

Though it is usually called the parable of the prodigal son, I call it the story of the two sons, since it is about *two* sons, not one. I call it a story, not a parable, not to deny that it is a parable but to respect the fact that Luke 15:3 seems to refer to all three stories found in Luke 15 as a single parable. Here is the chapter as a whole:

Now all the tax collectors and sinners were drawing near to hear him. And the Pharisees and the scribes were grumbling, saying, "This man receives sinners and eats with them." And he told

1 According to the *Tyndale House Greek New Testament*.

them this parable, saying, "What man of you, having a hundred sheep, if he loses one of them, does not leave the ninety-nine in the wilderness and go after the one that is lost until he finds it? And when he has found it, he puts it on his shoulders, rejoicing. And when he has come home, he calls together his friends and neighbors, saying to them, 'Rejoice with me, for I have found my sheep that was lost.' I tell you that thus there will be more joy in heaven over one sinner who repents than over ninety-nine righteous persons who have no need of repentance.

"Or what woman, having ten drachmas, if she loses one drachma, does not light a lamp and sweep the house and seek diligently until she finds it? And when she has found it, she calls together her friends and neighbors, saying, 'Rejoice with me, for I have found the drachma that I had lost.' Thus, I tell you, there is joy before the angels of God over one sinner who repents."

And he said, "A certain man had two sons. And the younger of them said to his father, 'Father, give me the share of possessions that is coming to me.' And he divided his livelihood between them. And not many days later, the younger son gathered everything and took a journey into a far country, and there he squandered his possessions living dissolutely. And when he had spent everything, there arose a severe famine in that country, and he began to be in need. And he went and attached himself to one of the citizens of that country, and he sent him into his fields to feed pigs. And he was longing to be filled with the pods that the pigs ate, and no one was giving him anything. But coming to himself, he said, 'How many of my father's hired servants have more than enough bread, but I am perishing here with hunger! I will arise and go to my father, and I will say to him, "Father, I have sinned against heaven and before you. I am no longer worthy to be called your son. Make me like one of your hired servants.'" And he arose and came to his father. But while he was still far off, his father saw him and felt compassion, and ran and fell on his neck and kissed him. And the son said to him, 'Father, I have sinned against heaven and before you. I am no longer worthy to be called your son.' But the father said to his servants, 'Quick! Bring out the best robe, and put it on him, and put a ring on his hand and shoes on his feet. And bring the fattened calf and kill it, and let us eat and celebrate. For this my son was dead and is alive again; he was lost and is found.' And they began to celebrate. Now his older son was in the field, and when he came and drew near to the house, he heard music and dancing. And he called one of the lads and asked what these things meant. And he said to him, 'Your brother has come, and your father has killed the fattened calf, because he has received him back in good health.' But he was angry and was not willing to go in. And his father came out and entreated him, but he answered his father, 'Look, all these years I have slaved for you, and I never disobeyed your command, and you never gave me a young goat that I might celebrate with my friends. But when this son of yours came, who has devoured your livelihood with prostitutes, you killed the fattened calf for him!' And he said to him, 'Child, you are always with me, and all my things are yours. But it was necessary to celebrate and be glad, for this your brother was dead and is alive again, and he was lost and is found.'"

After the introductory sentence, "A certain man had two sons" (5 Greek words), the story divides between the account of the younger son (239 words) and the older son (144 words).[2] As the younger son takes up about 62 percent of the story and the older son a mere 38 percent, it is natural that the whole is often named after the younger son alone.[3] The story is a single paragraph in our earliest copy, which reflects the fact that when the storyteller told this story, he did not pause between the sections about the two contrasting sons.[4] Yet the content may be read in two sections, each ending with the father saying that the younger son "was dead and is alive again, and he was lost and is found" (Luke 15:24, 32).[5] Even though the storyteller does not pause, there is still a clear literary structure.

The story is one of several parables that occur in Luke's Gospel alone and is part of a series of three stories in Luke 15:

1. The first story tells of one hundred sheep, with one lost and then found.
2. The second tells of ten coins, with one lost and then found.
3. The third tells of two sons, of whom only one is explicitly said to be lost and then found.

Not only are the three stories connected by being about things lost and found, they all contain celebrations and parallel

---

2 The story never calls them the "younger brother" or "older brother." I therefore generally call them "younger son" and "older son," though, of course, it is not wrong to note their brotherhood, which is an important aspect of the story.

3 This already occurred in the running head of the King James Version (1611 original), which named this section "The lost sheepe and prodigall sonne."

4 The earliest manuscript of this passage is Hanna Papyrus 1 (Mater Verbi) in the Vatican Library, also known as Papyrus 75, usually dated to the third century. Images of Hanna Papyrus 1 are available at https://digi.vatlib.it/view/MSS_Pap.Hanna.1(Mater.Verbi). It divides the whole of Luke 15 into just three paragraphs, as reflected in my translation above.

5 The Greek wording of the two verses varies slightly.

each other, with the first two seeming to be a "warm-up act" for the third. It is not just that the first two stories are much shorter than the third; they also prepare for it since in the first story the sheep gets lost by *going away* and in the second the coin gets lost *at home*. The third and final story then tells of the younger son who, like the sheep, gets lost by *going away* but then of the older son who, like the coin, has not left home. So we have artistry in the three individual stories and also artistry in the way they hang together and enrich each other. The implication of the three stories together is that the older son too is lost.

As the numbers in the stories become smaller, moving from one hundred to ten to two, the focus increases. The stories of the lost sheep and the lost coin, which were probably equivalent in value, are preparing us for the longest story, which is about the most valuable lost entity, namely, humans. In the first story, 1 percent of the flock is lost and found; in the second, 10 percent of the wealth is lost and found; and in the third story, 100 percent of the sons are lost, although we have often thought of only the younger son as lost. At least one, 50 percent, is found, but the question is left open about whether the other one will be found too.[6]

The Audiences

Luke's Gospel portrays the story of the two sons as being told in a particular historical setting. This is described in the first two verses of Luke 15:

6 I am grateful to my friend and fellow Tyndale House researcher James Bejon for insights underlying this paragraph.

Now all the tax collectors and sinners were drawing near to hear him. And the Pharisees and the scribes were grumbling, saying, "This man receives sinners and eats with them." (15:1–2)

According to Luke, besides Jesus's disciples, four sets of people were present, described in two groups:

1. Tax collectors and sinners: Tax collectors were typically Jews who collaborated with the occupying Romans or their puppet rulers in collecting money and were therefore unpopular.[7] People were probably called "sinners" because they consistently flouted rules—both rules from the Mosaic law and rules from later traditions.

2. Pharisees and scribes: Pharisees, whose name means "separated ones," were the largest religiously defined subgroup within Judaism and were characterized by their knowledge of the Jewish law and by their strong desire to maintain ritual purity through observing rules.[8] The scribes were particularly tasked with the meticulous copying of the Jewish Scriptures and therefore would have known those texts intimately.[9] This last point is important, for we will see that Jesus's challenge would have pushed their wits to the limit.

---

7 Tax collectors were not always viewed as apostate from Judaism. One of them was chosen as part of an important delegation of Jewish leaders to negotiate peace with the Romans. Josephus, *Jewish War* 2.287, 292. See Fritz Herrenbrück, *Jesus und die Zöllner: Historische und neutestamentlich-exegetische Untersuchungen*, WUNT 2nd ser., vol. 41 (Tübingen: J. C. B. Mohr, 1990), 211–13.

8 Josephus, *Jewish Antiquities* 17.41–42.

9 From Mark 12:38–40 we see that Jewish scribes could also be cultural leaders.

According to Luke's Gospel, itself a work of skill, the group of religious outcasts was "drawing near" to Jesus to "hear" him. "Hear" is the final word of the preceding chapter, which ends with Jesus's saying "Let the one who has ears to hear, *hear*" (14:35). Devout Jewish men back then would recite the most famous Jewish prayer, the Shema, every day, as many still do in our time. The Shema is named after its first word, "hear," from Deuteronomy 6:4: "Hear, O Israel: The LORD our God, the LORD is one." So we have a picture of the nondevout group being the ones who are devoutly *listening* to Jesus. They are also said to be "drawing near" to Jesus and thus are far closer to the teacher God has sent than are those who claim to be pious.

Meanwhile, the supposedly devout group of Pharisees and scribes are "grumbling," a term loaded with the memory that Israel repeatedly grumbled while they wandered for forty years in the wilderness (Ex. 15:24; 16:2; 17:3; Num. 14:2; 16:11, 41). "Hearing" and "grumbling" are opposite reactions, showing us the piety of the impious and the impiety of the pious. Everything is reversed.

The Pharisees and scribes are grumbling about the company Jesus keeps. Their complaint in Luke 15:2 is "This man receives sinners and eats with them." They were scrupulous not to eat with the religiously impure. It is in response to their charge that Jesus is eating with the wrong people that he reportedly tells the three stories of what was lost and then found.

As we have our first run through the story of the two sons, even on the surface it should be apparent that the storyteller has skillfully expressed a lot with an economy of words.

Scene 1 (Luke 15:11–24)

The story begins,

> A certain man had two sons. (Luke 15:11)

Already in these opening words, we have hallmarks of Jesus's speech since another parable attributed to Jesus in Matthew 21:28–32 begins the same way: "What do you think? A man had two sons." In that other parable, two sons are sent by their father to work in the vineyard. One refuses at first and later goes; the other agrees at first but then does not go. That story, like the one here, was told to show that sometimes tax collectors and those known for their sins were closer to God than the apparently righteous (Matt. 21:32). So we have two different stories with the same opening in two different Gospels, but both make the same point. That is naturally explained if they came from the same person.

As soon as we hear this opening to Jesus's story, we expect the two sons to be rather different, which is just how they turn out to be. The tale continues:

> And the younger of them said to his father, "Father, give me the share of possessions that is coming to me." And he divided his livelihood between them. (Luke 15:12)

This verse is one of the most important to grasp. I have taught this story on many occasions and asked the audience what the father did when the younger son demanded his inheritance. The usual reply is "He gave it to him." But it says he divided his possessions "between *them*."

This is a fair-minded father, who will not give the younger son his inheritance without also giving the older son his share. So the older son does rather well. The storyteller leaves to our imagination where this story takes place. Nevertheless, the story is addressed to Jews, and in Jewish law the firstborn son received a special inheritance, which was double that of his brothers (Deut. 21:17). Since they appear to be on a farm estate and the younger son goes away only with possessions that can be moved, we might even assume that all the real estate goes to the older son and that the younger son gets only a share of the movable possessions. Whether or not that is so, Jewish hearers of this story would have imagined the older son receiving most of the father's wealth. This sets the background to the reaction of the older son later in the story.

And now we have a single verse, which could easily be made into an entire film:

> And not many days later, the younger son gathered everything and took a journey into a far country, and there he squandered his possessions living dissolutely. (Luke 15:13)

Later in the story we see that the family must be reasonably wealthy since they have both hired and domestic servants, fine clothes, and a calf already fattened for a feast. Now this younger son has plenty of wealth and wastes it in reckless living.

The word "waste" or "squander"—in Greek, *diaskorpizō* (δια-σκορπίζω)—is significant. It is not a particularly common word but occurs again in the immediately following context, namely, the first verse of the next chapter, where we read,

> He [Jesus] also said to the disciples, "There was a rich man who had a manager, and charges were brought to him that this man was *wasting* his possessions." (16:1)

So we have two adjacent stories about people *wasting possessions*. What is more, we are told that the Pharisees did not like what they heard:

> The Pharisees, who were lovers of money, heard all these things, and they ridiculed him. (16:14)

If you are a hard worker, then you probably hate wastefulness. The Pharisees were generally hardworking in their business and donated with relative generosity to various causes. Jesus, of course, does not criticize conscientious work, but he does criticize an attitude common among those who work most diligently. Hard workers know that serious work pays and that reward follows effort, and in their mind there is often a law: work leads to reward, but sin and waste have disastrous consequences.[10] Very readily, a working person concludes that he or she is reaping the rewards of his or her own goodness and that those who do not work as much are reaping the rewards of their own badness. Self-righteousness can come easily to a hard worker.

These two stories about wasters are thus rather provocative since their central characters waste money and yet are supposed

---

10 Many verses in Proverbs support this idea, such as Prov. 10:4; 12:24, 27; 13:4; 21:5.

to depict something about God's kingdom. The experience of the wasteful son shows clearly that people who have wasted all that God has given them are welcome to return to him and to be accepted fully as his children.

The story of the two sons hits the mark because hard workers can easily feel indignant at the actions of those who work less hard. In a religious context, hard workers may consider themselves closer to God. This story raises the possibility that those who have more obviously failed in religious matters may have a clearer grasp of God's free grace and forgiveness. Jesus even says elsewhere that the person forgiven the greater debt may love more (7:41–50).

A whole lifestyle is encapsulated in the single word I have translated "dissolutely" (15:13).[11] We wish the storyteller would say more, but our wish is denied. Unlike subsequent retellings, the story has nothing to say about any wild parties this man may or may not have thrown. Details of his wasteful life are left entirely to the imagination, which is the most powerful place for them to be. It takes a good storyteller to know what to omit. By omitting such details, the storyteller avoids restricting our thoughts to one particular vice and steers clear of any glorification of such a lifestyle.

But just when the younger son runs out of money, disaster strikes:

And when he had spent everything, there arose a severe famine in that country, and he began to be in need. (15:14)

11 For a papyrus using similar phraseology to describe the financially wasteful living of a young man in Egypt, see G. Milligan, *Selections from the Greek Papyri* (Cambridge: Cambridge University Press, 1910), 71–72.

It seems quite coincidental, at least on the surface level of the story, that a severe famine hits at this moment. A *severe famine* might be distinguished from a mere *famine* by occurring over multiple years. Anyway, this significant famine is a clever part of the story. One scholar has shown that it tends to be forgotten when people from contexts untouched by hunger think of this account. Those who forget this part of the story attribute all the blame for the younger son's wretchedness to his own actions.[12] But with perfect balance, this story shows that it is a combination of bad choices plus bad "luck" that leads to the son's misery. He is unlucky enough to choose the one country hit by the famine: "There arose a severe famine *in that country*" (15:14). His bad luck is rather important later (in 15:30), when the older son attributes the younger son's ruin *entirely* to his own actions.

The story continues, recounting the man's wretchedness:

> And he went and attached himself to one of the citizens of that country, and he sent him into his fields to feed pigs. And he was longing to be filled with the pods that the pigs ate, and no one was giving him anything. (15:15–16)

Now in a tight spot, he next moves to get what could loosely be called a "job." The phrase I have translated "attached himself to" (ESV: "hired himself out to") does not say that someone hires him; it makes clear that he receives no pay. A more literal rendering of the key verb *ekollēthē* (ἐκολλήθη) would be "he stuck to." We

---

12 Mark Allan Powell, "The Forgotten Famine: Personal Responsibility in Luke's Parable of 'the Prodigal Son,'" in *Literary Encounters with the Reign of God*, ed. Sharon H. Ringe and H. C. Paul Kim (New York: T&T Clark, 2004), 265–87.

might imagine the younger son so desperate that he hangs around a citizen, who is prepared to take advantage of his desperate offer of free labor but gives him no pay. Note also the skillful choice of the word "citizen" here, poignantly emphasizing that whereas this local has status and a country, the younger son does not.

The storyteller's choice of pig herding as the man's job is powerful. It was one of the worst jobs he could do. For Jews, shepherding was not a prestigious job, but pig herding was far worse since it combined the low status of herding with the ritual uncleanness of pigs.[13] If this really were told to the audience described in Luke's Gospel, it would work well psychologically. We could imagine that a Pharisee listening to the story at this point would be pleased that things were working out badly for this waster. Any member of the audience who liked to see sinners get what they deserve would have been on board—before the story turned and pointed at them.[14]

The pigs eat pods, which are scarcely digestible for humans, but the man is not even able to obtain these. So the story has brought us to a point at which the man is utterly desperate and at risk of dying of hunger. The storyteller has portrayed hunger, loneliness, shame, and uncleanness as the man reaches rock bottom.

Then something changes. But rather than describing how he comes to his senses, our narrator cleverly gives us a view into the man's mind, as we hear his self-address:

13 In the family King David grew up in, it was the job that could be left to the youngest brother when older brothers were called to something more important (see 1 Sam. 16:11). The Greek historian Herodotus (ca. 484–ca. 425 BC) also tells of how in Egypt swineherds were viewed as especially unclean. Herodotus, *Histories* 2.47. One rabbinic saying was "Cursed is the one who raises pigs and cursed is the one who teaches his son Greek wisdom." Babylonian Talmud Menahot 64b.

14 See Kenneth E. Bailey, *Finding the Lost: Cultural Keys to Luke 15* (St. Louis, MO: Concordia, 1992), 127.

But coming to himself, he said, "How many of my father's hired servants have more than enough bread, but I am perishing here with hunger! I will arise and go to my father, and I will say to him, 'Father, I have sinned against heaven and before you. I am no longer worthy to be called your son. Make me like one of your hired servants.'" (15:17–19)

Thus the younger son returns to sanity, recognizing that even the father's temporary paid laborers, without job security, are far better off than him. He acknowledges his sin and is prepared to ask to be accepted simply as a servant rather than as a son.

Then the journey from the pigsty to the father's kiss takes just a single verse:

And he arose and came to his father. But while he was still far off, his father saw him and felt compassion, and ran and fell on his neck and kissed him. (15:20)

The father's response, while unsurprising to any who have heard the story before, is deeply counter to what first-time hearers expect in multiple ways. Whereas by his actions the younger son has renounced his family, publicly shamed his father, and squandered much of his estate, we see various surprises:

1. The father saw him a long way off, which suggests that he had been regularly scanning the horizon, yearning for the younger son to return.
2. The father runs. He is a man with adult children, and the younger son has been away for a considerable time (15:29).

It is reasonable to imagine him as quite old and of a dignity such that running would be rather beneath him.[15]

3. The father's first reaction is "compassion," not anger.
4. The younger son is welcomed back publicly and unconditionally to his former status.

Next, the younger son begins his speech:

And the son said to him, "Father, I have sinned against heaven and before you. I am no longer worthy to be called your son." (15:21)

If we compare this speech with the soliloquy of Luke 15:18–19, we see that he gets only halfway through what he had planned to say. He does not get to the part about being a servant. The storyteller makes us wonder why, and most who hear the story conclude that the father has interrupted him.[16] The skillfulness of the story is in implying this without saying it explicitly.

Next, the father speaks, but surprisingly, he does not address his son. In fact, he never addresses the younger son, though later he addresses the older son. There is literally no need for him to say anything to the younger son. Positive speech such as "Welcome" or "I love you" is not necessary since the father's actions—his run, his embrace, and his kiss—have spoken clearly. The father has no

---

15 See Bailey, *Finding the Lost*, 144.

16 In some significant manuscripts (Vaticanus, fourth century; Sinaiticus, fourth century; Bezae, fifth century), he does get to complete the speech and says, "Make me as one of your hired servants," in Luke 15:21. Many different manuscripts, however, line up to support the omission of these words, and it seems likely that these words were simply added by copyists based on 15:19.

thought of reprimand or even of asking questions. Strikingly, the father's first words are to the servants, whose presence the able storyteller knew he did not need to announce.

> But the father said to his servants, "Quick! Bring out the best robe, and put it on him, and put a ring on his hand and shoes on his feet. And bring the fattened calf and kill it, and let us eat and celebrate. For this my son was dead and is alive again; he was lost and is found." And they began to celebrate. (15:22–24)

Although the ESV ("Bring quickly the best robe . . .") does not bring this out, the very first word to come out of the father's mouth is the Greek word *tachy* (ταχύ), "quick(ly)." Literally, he says, "Quick! Bring the first [i.e., best] robe, and put it on him." The first word is significant. For many years the father must have felt that time was moving incredibly slowly. Now, however, there is not a moment to lose. Wasted time in the past is now irrelevant, and the father intends to make up for lost time with speed. He gives commands that publicly transform his son's status—the robe and the ring demonstrating to everyone that the younger son has been restored to his former status.[17] Note that he is given the *highest-ranking* robe. Obviously, if he is wearing it, no one else can wear it, including the older son, who no doubt seems to have a better claim to it.

The younger son imagined he might be given bread (15:17), but in fact, the fattened calf is killed. Just one calf at a time is

---

17 Kenneth E. Bailey, *Jacob and the Prodigal: How Jesus Retold Israel's Story* (Downers Grove, IL: InterVarsity Press, 2003), 174.

fattened for slaughter, and it is kept for a special occasion. Thus the wastrel gets the best robe and the finest feast because the father commands it.

Within the story, of course, both the best robe and the fattened calf legally belong to the older son since the father had given away all his possessions without remainder to his two sons. But the father's position as head of the family as well as legal convention would give him authority to use all the wealth of the farm during his lifetime, with the restriction that he could not dispose of the capital.[18] This gives him continued say over things that he has given away. Hearers may well feel uncomfortable at the father's generosity, but that discomfort is a deliberate feature of the story. The father's generosity *is* uncomfortable.

Having commanded the celebration, the father explains why they must celebrate: "This my son was dead and is alive again; he was lost and is found" (15:24). Being lost and found is a theme that runs right through this chapter (15:6, 9, 32). The storyteller says they *began* to celebrate, thus concisely hinting that the celebrations were likely to last long.

Scene 2 (Luke 15:25–32)

We now have a second scene. The older son, who has been entirely in the background in the first scene, now takes center stage.

Now his older son was in the field, and when he came and drew near to the house, he heard music and dancing. And he called one of the lads and asked what these things meant. And

18 This understanding is based on the Jewish rules written down around AD 200 in Mishnah, Bava Batra 8.7. See also Bailey, *Finding the Lost*, 116–17.

he said to him, "Your brother has come, and your father has killed the fattened calf, because he has received him back in good health." (Luke 15:25–27)

The older son is said to have been in the field. Listeners naturally infer that he was working late at a time when others were back at the house. He "drew near" to the house (15:25). The verb "drew near" is *ēngisen* (ἤγγισεν), from *engizō* (ἐγγίζω). Attentive listeners to Luke's Gospel remember that the sinners were "drawing near," *engizontes* (ἐγγίζοντες), also from *engizō* (ἐγγίζω), to Jesus (15:1), and the younger son went to a country that was "far," *makran* (μακράν, 15:13), and was seen "far off," also *makran* (μακράν, 15:20). Proximity and distance are key ideas, both for this story and for the wider setting in Luke. The younger son has been *far*, and the older son is now *close*. Even with these spatial words, the storyteller is doing a lot of work—deftly showing that physical distance is sometimes the opposite of the closeness of the relationship.

Next, the older son asks a servant for the reason for the music and dancing. He is given a prosaically factual reply: "Your brother has come, and your father has killed the fattened calf, because he has received him back in good health" (15:27). The servant reports bare facts, and we cannot tell what, if any, emotions he has about the matter. But the older son's reaction that follows is highly emotional:

But he was angry and was not willing to go in. And his father came out and entreated him, but he answered his father, "Look, all these years I have slaved for you, and I never disobeyed your command, and you never gave me a young goat that I might celebrate with my friends. But when this son of yours came, who has devoured your livelihood with prostitutes, you killed the fattened calf for him!" And he said to him, "Child, you are always with me, and all my things are yours. But it was necessary to celebrate and be glad, for this your brother was dead and is alive again, and he was lost and is found." (15:28–32)

Now we have the older son's response to the situation—anger, which contrasts with the compassion of the father. We might have expected a brother to have more understanding or even to be closer to his own sibling. The older son has done well financially from receiving his inheritance early. But he refuses to go in, so the father has to go out. In this case the older son is first to speak and is uninterrupted. It is worth weighing his words carefully.

He opens his speech with the word "Look." This alerts us to something we may have overlooked in the story: on three occasions the younger son addresses his father as "Father." Two of these occasions are in real life, and the other is as he rehearses his speech in his mind (15:12, 18, 21). The younger son always acknowledges the father *as his father*, even though his early actions in demanding his share and leaving home look like a public rejection of him. This highlights the absence of the word "father" at the beginning of the older son's angry outburst. He is supposedly the model son, but the absence of this word shows that, though physically closer to the father, he is relationally more distant than the younger son ever was. The storyteller conveys all this through just one missing word.

The older son's complaint continues:

All these years I have slaved for you. (15:29)

If any person had the right to use the phrase "all these years," it was surely the father. He could have complained to the younger son about "all these years" he had been away. Here, however, the older son sees his service as having lasted many years.

The word I have translated "I have slaved" comes from the verb *douleuō* (δουλεύω). English translations often tamely render the word as "I have served." It conveys the idea that though the older son has the status of son, he thinks of himself as a mere *slave*. There is, of course, a problem with the claim that he has been working for the father because at the beginning of the story we learned that the father divided all his possessions between the two sons. This means that the older son has been working on a farm that he himself owns. Every time that he has worked late, he has been building up his own wealth since the estate is already his. He speaks as if he has been a slave, but all along he has been a son. We get the impression that this is the first time that the older son has complained, but it is clearly not the first time he has *felt* like complaining. This phrase reveals the long-cherished resentment in his heart.

He continues:

I never disobeyed your command. (15:29)

This has a ring of truth to it. We can imagine that the older son was a model of outward obedience. But his words also depict the father as parenting through imperatives, which again probably reflects the older son's distorted perspective on the relationship. His obedience is purely negative: he did not break rules, but there is no evidence that he loved or respected his father.

It is similar to the narrative in Luke 18:18–27, in which Jesus is approached by a rich ruler wanting to inherit eternal life who claims to have kept all the commandments from his youth, yet he cannot face Jesus's command to sell all he has and give to the poor and thus receive treasure in heaven. Here too we have someone in the grip of materialism who thinks he has not broken the rules.

The older son continues:

> You never gave me a young goat that I might celebrate with my friends. (15:29)

The storyteller knows that it is hard for us to imagine that for all those years the older son has had no meat. He is complaining that he has not even been given a young goat, an animal a mere fraction of the size of the fattened calf that has just been killed.[19] He specifically complains that he was not given a young goat "that I might celebrate with my friends." Again, in line with the storyteller's skill, the significance of the phrase comes from *what is unstated.*

Who is on the older son's ideal guest list? Answer: himself and his friends. But the more penetrating question is this: Who is *not* on his guest list? Since he has presumably been regularly eating with the father and has usual social interaction with friends, including the ability to invite them to eat at the farm he himself

---

19 Note to townsfolk: young goats are preferred over old ones, since their meat is more tender.

owns, only one answer makes sense: *the older son does not want the father on the guest list*. All those times he has eaten meat with his father have not satisfied him. He wants the party with just his friends and himself. His words imply that he has no relationship with his father.

The older son also uses the word *celebrate*, a theme word in the three stories in Luke 15. The shepherd, the woman, and the father all *celebrate* when they find what was lost, just as heaven celebrates over finding a lost sinner. The older son, however, wants a completely different sort of celebration. His celebration with his friends and a mere young goat to eat is obviously inferior to the father's party with the fattened calf, which also implies an invitation wide enough to consume such a beast.[20]

The older son, however, would still prefer to remain outside the superior celebration. The shepherd, the woman, and the father all have *inclusive* celebrations: everyone is welcome, and they are celebrating the finding of what was lost. The shepherd and the woman invite both friends and neighbors. The father even explicitly invites the servants to enjoy meat and celebrate ("Let us eat and celebrate," 15:23). By contrast, the older son wants an *exclusive* celebration, with his select friends but not with his neighbors—and especially not with his father.

The older son continues his tirade:

> But when this son of yours came, who has devoured your livelihood with prostitutes, you killed the fattened calf for him! (15:30)

---

20 Even a modest-size fattened calf yielding 450 lb. of beef would supply hundreds of portions of meat.

The older son concludes his complaint by referring to "this son of yours." As elsewhere in the story, the force of the phrase is in its implicit denial. By not saying "my brother," he is in effect denying the reality of his relationship with his brother.

Next, he complains about how his nonbrother has devoured their father's livelihood "with prostitutes." Obviously, the younger son has not devoured *all* the father's livelihood since there they are on the farm. Besides which the older son has received at least half the father's possessions for himself—and quite probably more. So the older son is exaggerating the damage to the father, and there is no reason to think that he cares about his father's welfare and every reason to think that he cares about his own.

What about the reference to prostitutes? How can the older son know what his brother did in a distant country? He has not seen him since his return and is himself only just back from the field. The natural way to hear the story is that there has been no communication of any kind from the younger son. Alternative scenarios are, of course, imaginable, but the story gives us no hint that they are likely. As for the father, the younger son has been effectively "dead." Therefore, the most probable source of the older son's "information" that his younger brother frequented prostitutes is his own imagination.[21] The storyteller wisely does not give us the unedifying details of the younger son's misdemeanors. So the older son's conviction that his brother's most significant expense has been with prostitutes could indicate that prostitutes may have occupied his own imagination.

---

21 "The accusation of immorality stems from the imagination of the older brother, not from the narrator of the story." Bailey, *Finding the Lost*, 123.

We see the warped perspective further reflected in the older son's claim "You killed the fattened calf *for him*." Of course, it is not just "for him"; everyone can enjoy the meat.

Then we have the father's final word, with which the story ends:

And he said to him, "Child, you are always with me, and all my things are yours. But it was necessary to celebrate and be glad, for this your brother was dead and is alive again, and he was lost and is found." (15:31–32)

He addresses him as "child," which is what he truly is. The older son has twice used the word "never," *oudepote* (οὐδέποτε), saying, "I *never* disobeyed your command," and, "You *never* gave me a young goat" (15:29). The father here replies with the related word "always," *pantote* (πάντοτε), saying, "You are always with me." He says that all that he has belongs to his older son, which is quite literally true. But he explains that there is no choice about celebrating. The father responds to the phrase "this son of yours," *ho huios sou houtos* (ὁ υἱός σου οὗτος), with the related phrase "this brother of yours," *ho adelphos sou houtos* (ὁ ἀδελφός σου οὗτος). The return of his brother from death to life, from being lost to being found, is so dramatic that celebration is obligatory.

The story stops here, not telling us whether the older son softened in response to the father's final words. The open-ended nature of the story serves to invite people like him not to stay outside the celebration. Since the preceding stories of a sheep *lost away from home* and of a coin *lost at home* both ended in celebration, it follows that there would be celebration for the spiritual restoration of the older son *lost at home*, as there is of the younger son *lost away from home*. This is not stated on the surface. Rather, like in a sudoku, the storyteller leaves gaps that have to be filled in by the audience while giving enough clues for them to fill those gaps in correctly. But the story also ends without any positive sign from the older son. This detail highlights the fact that without a radical change of attitude, the older son, like the Pharisees and scribes, will remain outside the celebration.

Short and Strong

The story of the two sons is short and can be read at a leisurely pace in English in just two and a half minutes. It is a powerful story in any setting for what it conveys about some of the closest human family relationships, about money, and about authority and our desire for independence. It deals with anger, greed, love, resentment, and shame—even before we consider its wider scope in handling human relationships with God. For these reasons alone, the story ought to stand out in any talent show.

Yet it is even *more* powerful when considered in the context in which it is reported, with tax collectors, sinners, Pharisees, and scribes all present. It would have been rhetorically forceful because tax collectors and sinners seem to align with the younger son, and Pharisees and scribes with the older son, and yet the younger son was the one clearly reconciled to his father, who is rather analogous to God. Originating from that context, it retains its power also across many subsequent cultural contexts, in which established groups have assumed that they have a greater share of God's favor.

There is another feature of the story's power: the text in Luke 15 often conveys significantly more than is on the surface of its words.

1. "Citizens" in 15:15 highlights the younger son's non-citizen status.
2. "Pigs" in 15:15 highlights his ritual uncleanness.
3. "Look" in 15:29 highlights the older son's failure to use the word "father."
4. "That I might celebrate with my friends" in 15:29 implies not celebrating with his father.
5. "This son of yours" in 15:30 implies a disowning of his brother.
6. The older son's conviction about what his brother has been doing reveals his own sinful imagination.
7. Ending the story without giving the response of the older son highlights the need for those who align with him to respond the right way.

To convey all this in under four hundred words is a work of great artistry of the kind that, I hope you will agree, displays *genius*. In the following pages, however, we see that beneath the surface are layers of deeper meaning in the story, which show it to be cleverer still. These layers support the idea that the story genuinely comes from Jesus himself and was told to the very people mentioned in Luke. I argue not only that the story has been transmitted with integrity from Jesus but also that the historical setting of the story has been well transmitted too.

Jesus's audience consisted of tax collectors, sinners, Pharisees, and scribes. Pharisees were supposed to be enthusiasts for the law of Moses, and scribes spent much of their time copying out scriptures, especially the Torah, also known as the Pentateuch—the first five books of the Bible, from Genesis to Deuteronomy. In what follows we see that the story has layers of meaning that are unlocked only when one considers the story of God's people as told in the first book of the Bible, Genesis.

2

Connecting with Genesis

A KEY GROUP in Jesus's audience for the story of the two sons was the scribes. Though they may not have spent all their time copying religious texts (they probably provided legal services too), they were clearly deeply familiar with the Jewish Scriptures. By the time of Jesus's ministry, scribes had introduced very careful textual controls to ensure the correct transmission of the authorized Torah text. Our best evidence for such scribal practices at the time comes from the Dead Sea Scrolls. These are a great source of information, even if the group that collected them was on the social margins of Judaism.

The Dead Sea Scrolls contain high-quality biblical manuscripts made to strict copying standards as well as less formally produced manuscripts. In the high-quality copies, the exact spelling of words is defined, even though in other contexts there may have been more than one way to spell those words. Over time, to help scribes preserve the exact spelling of words and the exact wording of phrases, scribes invented elaborate systems of counting and labeling letters. The labeling systems then became part of scribal training. The Dead

Sea Scrolls show that some such scribal signs had begun to develop by the time of Jesus, though there were not nearly as many as there would be in the heyday of the Masoretes, the famous copyists active from the fifth to tenth centuries AD. In order to produce the most careful copies, scribes of Jesus's day would have had to be very familiar with the precise wording of Genesis.[1]

My argument is that Jesus's story echoes details from most of the major stories in Genesis. Whether or not they recognized this, the Pharisees and scribes were being presented simultaneously both with evidence of Jesus's deep understanding of Genesis and with moral challenges arising from its narratives.

Sometimes in addition to similarities between Jesus's story and stories in Genesis, we actually see contrasts, so that what happens in Jesus's story is the opposite of what happens in Genesis. It seems likely that Jesus used both similarities and contrasts to make points to his opponents.

In what follows, we explore the echoes of Genesis as layers of meaning, and I present them in the order in which I first became aware of them, in the hope that this means that I deal with the more obvious layers first.

Jacob and Esau

Jesus's story begins:

A certain man had two sons. (Luke 15:11)

---

1 Genesis was a particularly popular book. It is the Torah book most frequently used by the Jewish historian Josephus (ca. AD 37–ca. 100) and the book most treated by Philo (ca. 20 BC–ca. AD 50), the leading Alexandrian Jewish writer of the time. If we include works based on it, like 1 Enoch and Jubilees, alongside manuscripts of the book itself, Genesis is also the most represented work among the Dead Sea Scrolls.

The question for an expert scribe is this: Where in the Bible do we get a story about a man who has two sons? The two answers I most commonly get from an audience are (1) Abraham, who has Ishmael and Isaac, and (2) Isaac, who has Esau and Jacob. The fact that audiences come up with both of these suggestions shows that they are actually both good replies.

In Genesis, Abraham and his wife, Sarah, are too old to have children, and yet God promises them a son, at first stating merely that the child will be Abraham's (Gen. 15:4) and later further specifying that the boy will also come from his wife, Sarah (17:16). In the time between these two promises, Abraham and Sarah try to bring about the fulfillment of the promise of a son to Abraham by having him sleep with Sarah's Egyptian maidservant Hagar. From this union Ishmael is born. Consequently, Abraham becomes a man with two sons: Ishmael and Isaac, the former born from a servant and the latter born from a free woman. But though several passages contrast the two sons, Abraham does not have *only two sons*. After Sarah dies, he takes another wife, Keturah, and has six more sons by her, though they scarcely feature within the narrative (25:1–6). So Abraham is certainly a candidate for a man with two sons, but Isaac is an even better fit.

Isaac is by far the most famous man in the Old Testament to have two *and only two* sons. He has Esau and Jacob, from the same mother, Rebekah. These two sons are also famous rivals who contrast significantly. Jacob, his mother's favorite, prefers the indoors, and Esau, his father's favorite, prefers the outdoors. Here is the first narrative we have about them.

When the boys grew up, Esau was a skillful hunter, a man of the field, while Jacob was a quiet man, dwelling in tents.

Isaac loved Esau because he ate of his game, but Rebekah loved Jacob.

Once when Jacob was cooking stew, Esau came in from the field, and he was exhausted. And Esau said to Jacob, "Let me eat some of that red stew, for I am exhausted!" (Therefore his name was called Edom.) Jacob said, "Sell me your birthright now." Esau said, "I am about to die; of what use is a birthright to me?" Jacob said, "Swear to me now." So he swore to him and sold his birthright to Jacob. Then Jacob gave Esau bread and lentil stew, and he ate and drank and rose and went his way. Thus Esau despised his birthright. (25:27–34 ESV)

We notice links between these two brothers and Luke 15. First, Esau, the older brother, connected with the field, comes in from the field when the food has already been prepared (Gen. 25:29), just like the older son in Luke 15:25. Second, Esau says he is dying of starvation (Gen. 25:32), just like the younger son in Luke 15:17. More strikingly, the younger brother, Jacob, takes advantage of his older brother's desperation and gets him to forgo his right to inherit. Thus, this Genesis story is also about a man with two sons, one of whom has managed to trick the other out of his inheritance.

The question of inheritance underlies the story in Luke 15. Once the younger son returns, having spent all his inheritance, the older son is naturally concerned that his brother will have to be sustained from his own portion of the inheritance.

In Genesis, however, things between the brothers get worse. Isaac grows old and becomes visually impaired, and he asks Esau to go out to hunt meat for him to taste so that he can bless Esau before he dies (Gen. 27:1–4). Their mother, Rebekah, overhears this plan but prefers Jacob, and so she plots to cook food and help Jacob pretend that he is his older brother, Esau, and thereby get the blessing. The food that Rebekah prepares consists of two young goats, the only time in the Hebrew Bible when goats are specifically recorded as a meal.[2] She also dresses Jacob in the older brother's *best robe* (27:9, 15). Isaac cannot see and so asks for his son to come close. A scribe would likely notice that the verb "draw near" is used *six times* in seven verses as Jacob draws near and brings food to his father (27:21–27). As a result of Jacob's successful trickery, Esau loses the blessing and is so murderously angry with his brother that Jacob must flee to a far country, where he does herding work for a relative before returning rather wealthy.

Thus we have at least ten things in common between Luke 15 and the story of Esau and Jacob: (1) a man with two sons, (2) a younger brother going into a far country, (3) the younger brother herding animals in that far country, (4) someone saying he is dying of hunger, (5) a younger brother wearing the best robes given by a parent, (6) an older brother coming in from a field,[3] (7) the use of the word "draw near" (Luke 15:25), (8) an older brother being angry, (9) concern about an older brother losing some inheritance to a younger one, and (10) young goats as a meal.

But set amid these connections is one connection that is particularly striking to any scribe because at this point there is a special match with the wording of Genesis.[4] When Jesus recounts the younger son's return, he says,

2 Kenneth E. Bailey, *Jacob and the Prodigal: How Jesus Retold Israel's Story* (Downers Grove, IL: InterVarsity Press, 2003), 188.

3 John Drury notes that Esau was in the field, like the older brother in Luke 15. *The Parables in the Gospels: History and Allegory* (London: SPCK, 1985), 145.

4 Otfried Hofius, "Alttestamentliche Motive im Gleichnis vom verlorenen Sohn," *New Testament Studies* 24, no. 2 (1978): 242–43.

But while he was still far off, his father saw him and felt compassion, and *ran* and *fell on his neck and kissed him*. (Luke 15:20)

To anyone trained in counting phrases who has copied out Genesis several times, this sentence is striking because there is only one other text in the entire Bible in which someone runs, falls on someone's neck, and kisses that person. These three actions occur when Esau welcomes his cheating younger brother, Jacob, back from a far country.

But Esau *ran* to meet him and embraced him and *fell on his neck and kissed him*, and they wept. (Gen. 33:4 ESV)

This verse should have been well known to every scribe because it was one of only fifteen places in the whole Bible where scribes had to add special dots above a word, most likely used to show a textual dispute. Scribes were specially trained to place six of these dots over the six letters of the word "and he kissed him," *vayyishshaqehu* (וַיִּשָּׁקֵהוּ), in Genesis 33:4 (see figure 1). That means that every scribe Jesus addresses in the story of the two sons had themselves placed these dots above the word in this verse.[5]

---

5   Though we do not have manuscripts with superimposed dots, or *puncta extraordinaria*, on the particular word *vayyishshaqehu* (וַיִּשָּׁקֵהוּ) in Gen. 33:4 from the time of Jesus, we have six converging lines of evidence that this practice was in place by Jesus's day. (1) We have examples of the early use of such dots but on different words among the Dead Sea Scrolls (such as the Great Isaiah Scroll, 1QIsaᵃ, from over a century before Jesus). (2) The dot over the letter *he* in Num. 9:10 (one of the ten examples of these points in the Pentateuch) is commented on by the mid-second-century rabbi Jose ben Halafta (Mishnah Pesahim 9.2). Rabbi Jose assumes that the dot is as much a part of the biblical text as the letters themselves and gives an implausible explanation for it, demonstrating that by his time the original purpose of the dot had been forgotten. (3) The existence of

Figure 1 Manuscript Or. 4445, folio 23v, from the Pentateuch. Dating from around AD 920–950, this manuscript, like the entire tradition of medieval Hebrew manuscripts, has dots, known as *puncta extraordinaria*, over each of the six letters of "and he kissed him" (וַיִּשָּׁקֵהוּ) in Gen. 33:4. © British Library Board. All rights reserved / Bridgeman Images.

---

dots in Gen. 33:4 is confirmed by the discussion in Sifre Num. 69.2. (4) These fifteen sets of dots occur in all the medieval manuscripts, both scrolls (which have few markings beyond the consonants) and codices (which are full of such markings). (5) The dots are found in both the Tiberian and the Babylonian consonantal scroll texts, showing that they were considered as much a part of the biblical text as the consonants themselves, which were available in a fixed form before the beginning of the Jewish War with Rome (AD 66). (6) We have a reference to the particular dots on "and he kissed him" in Gen. 33:4, which survives in an eleventh-century Greek Christian manuscript that comes from a tradition largely separate from the Jewish tradition: "The 'and he kissed him,' which in Hebrew is *ouessakē*, has dots on it in every Hebrew manuscript," *to katephilēsen aut(on) aper estin hebraisti. ouessakē en panti hebraikōi bibliōi periestiktai* (τὸ κατεφίλησεν αὐτ[ὸν] ἅπερ ἐστὶν ἑβραϊστὶ. οὐεσσακη ἐν παντὶ ἑβραϊκῶι βιβλίωι περιέστικται). Biblioteca Apostolica Vaticana, Vat. gr. 747, folio 55r; https://digi.vatlib.it/mss/detail/Vat.gr .747. For evidence that efforts to fix even the pronunciation of the biblical text go back before AD 70, see Geoffrey Khan, "Orthoepy in the Tiberian Reading Tradition of the Hebrew Bible and Its Historical Roots in the Second Temple Period," *Vetus Testamentum* 68 (2018): 378–401. For more about these dots, see Emanuel Tov, *Scribal Practices and Approaches Reflected in the Texts Found in the Judean Desert* (Leiden: Brill, 2004), 214–16. I am grateful to Benjamin Kantor and Kim Phillips for help in compiling this note.

Genesis 33:4 is also a huge surprise in its context. It is arguably the most unexpected response in the entire Old Testament. Jacob had tricked Esau out of his inheritance and blessing. As a result, Esau hated Jacob so much that he wanted to kill him (27:41). At this point Jacob is returning from a far country and has heard that Esau is coming to meet him with four hundred men. He fears the worst, and the preceding chapter, Genesis 32, is taken up with Jacob's plans to ensure that some of his people escape if Esau attacks. Against this backdrop, Esau's embrace is stunning.

So the most astonishing verse in Jesus's whole story—the father running, embracing, and kissing his younger son—comes from a verse that Jewish scribes knew particularly well. The image of the old father running not only is the most dramatic point in the entire story but also is based on one of the Old Testament verses that scribes had special rules for copying. The high point of the drama exactly matches a place of scribal interest.

But there is a further element of genius here. The storyteller has aligned the behavior of the father (who seems to represent God) with Esau, a man who has gone down in history as ungodly. This is a bold move for any storyteller. Yet it does make sense if one is a careful reader of Genesis since just six verses after Esau runs and falls on Jacob's neck and kisses him, Jacob declares that encountering Esau is like seeing the face of God (33:10).[6] So the

---

6 Hofius, "Alttestamentliche Motive," 246. The face of God is a theme in Genesis. Only thirteen verses earlier, Jacob names a place Peniel, meaning "face of God," after he encounters God there (Gen. 32:30). The resemblance between Esau and God in Genesis is argued by Brian Neil Peterson, "Jacob's Tithe: Did Jacob Keep His Vow to God?," *Journal of the Evangelical Theological Society* 63, no. 2 (2020): 255–65, esp. 262.

storyteller knows how to create drama in a story, how to have special impact on his target audience, and how to read the Old Testament with great care.

This story also contains some intriguing *contrasts* with the story of Esau and Jacob, which it is hard to believe are all coincidental. I have laid these out in table 1.

Table 1 Contrasts between the Jacob-Esau Story and the Story of the Two Sons

Jacob and Esau Story	Story of the Two Sons
Jacob goes out with nothing and comes back with great wealth.	The younger son goes out with great wealth and comes back with nothing.
Esau comes in from the field saying that he is about to die of hunger and longing for Jacob's soup (Gen. 25:29, 32–34).	The younger son is at risk of dying of starvation and is longing for food (Luke 15:14–17).
Isaac, the father, wants meat hunted by Esau and is tricked into having young goat by Jacob (Gen. 27:9).	The older son wants the meat of a young goat (Luke 15:29).
Isaac asks Jacob to come up close because he cannot see him (Gen. 27:21–22, 26–27).	The father sees the younger son afar off (Luke 15:20).

In the parable's context in Luke, it seems that Jesus is giving multiple clues to scribes who copy out these very Bible phrases to point them to Genesis's story of reversal. It is a biblical pattern that those first in line to inherit are not always the ones who do inherit.

To anyone who observes the links between the story of the two sons and the Jacob-Esau story, Jesus is making a powerful point: Esau goes down in biblical history as someone who prefers soup to God and whose descendants generally oppose Israel. Yet here Jesus uses Esau's reaction as the model for the father, who especially symbolizes God in the story.

Esau had reason to be angry, but he responded warmly to his brother's return. If even a person like Esau, who had previously planned to murder his brother, could accept his returning brother, how much more should the older son accept his brother? Esau was cheated out of *all* his inheritance as firstborn, but the older son is worried about a generous welcome for his brother, despite his own inheritance being secure.

But is it even right to conclude that the older son must be losing out? If we take a very narrow view of the resources available on a farm that appears to teem with abundance, then we might conclude that he does lose out. But that is also a distortion of reality. The older son's inheritance is secure and not at all threatened by the return of the younger son. He has access to the wealth of the estate, and though he might fear that his brother could survive only by scrounging off the estate, his fears are unfounded. The younger son's self-address has expressed his readiness to work. We who hear the story therefore know that we are most likely seeing the arrival of another worker to the farm. The older son cannot see this because he is mean-spirited and begrudges even the smallest allowance out of his abundance.

So even Esau, who is cheated out of all his inheritance, does not think in as mean a way as the older son. Likewise, the Pharisees and scribes should not resent that Jesus, and therefore God, welcomes tax collectors and sinners. They should not resent God's grace shown to the undeserving or react as if they stand to lose through God's generosity.

Only in the context in which the story is set in Luke does it make its full force felt. Pharisees, who were generally wealthy, would have resented the fact that tax collectors collaborated with Rome's representatives to take a cut of their wealth, sometimes dishonestly. Yet here we have a story showing that even Esau could teach them a lesson about forgiving someone who had ripped them off. Earlier, Esau had been waiting for his father, Isaac, to die so that he could take revenge on Jacob for cheating him out of his inheritance.

> Now Esau hated Jacob because of the blessing with which his father had blessed him, and Esau said to himself, "The days of mourning for my father are approaching; then I will kill my brother Jacob." (Gen. 27:41 ESV)

So Esau had wanted his father dead, just as the older son in Jesus's story wanted his father out of the way.

Now if all we had was a moving short story with a simple message and a number of parallels to and reversals of the Jacob-Esau story, it would be extremely impressive. But the story is a greater artistic feat, involving other echoes as well.[7]

Jacob and Laban

The story of the two sons also appears to contain allusions to the story of Jacob and his father-in-law, Laban. When Esau, his angry brother, threatens his life, Jacob, like the younger son, leaves home and goes to a far land—the country of his uncle Laban. There he works, looking

---

7 Bailey sees fifty-one common elements between Gen. 27:1–36:8 and the story of the two sons (Luke 15:11–32), which both overlap with and significantly differ from my analysis here. *Jacob and the Prodigal*, 210.

43

after Laban's flocks. Like the younger son, he initially works for no wages, but unlike the younger son, he is then able to get remuneration. An arrangement is made for him to be rewarded through marriage to Laban's beautiful daughter, Rachel, with whom Jacob is madly in love, in exchange for seven years of work.

Then there is a twist in the plot. Just as Jacob had tricked his blind father, Isaac, by pretending to be his older brother, Esau, so Jacob's uncle/father-in-law tricks him. In the blind darkness of Jacob's wedding night, Laban substitutes for Rachel his (apparently) less beautiful, older daughter, Leah. But Jacob still wants to marry Rachel and so ends up marrying both of Laban's daughters. In all, he works for Laban for twenty years, fourteen of which are in payment for his daughters, and the final six with payment in sheep. Genesis tells of his arrangement with Laban wherein Jacob gets to keep the speckled and spotted sheep while Laban keeps the rest. Over time, however, through his unconventional breeding methods, and even more through God's favor on him, Jacob gets an ever-larger number of sheep at Laban's expense. Jacob therefore decides to sneak away quietly. On the third day, Laban hears of his flight and pursues him, but before Laban catches up with Jacob, God explicitly tells Laban not to meddle with Jacob (Gen. 31:24).

The most obvious resemblance between this story and Luke 15 is that Jacob and the older son angrily complain of how they have worked for many years for their father-in-law or father, respectively. Jacob says angrily to his father-in-law,

> These twenty years I have been in your house. I served you four-
> teen years for your two daughters, and six years for your flock,
> and you have changed my wages ten times. (Gen. 31:41 ESV)

The older son angrily says to his father,

Look, all these years I have slaved for you. (Luke 15:29)

There are other fainter similarities and contrasts between the two stories:

1. Wealth as something eaten: Laban's daughters, Leah and Rachel, claim that Laban has "devoured" their wealth (Gen. 31:15), just as the older son claims that his younger brother has "devoured" the father's possessions with prostitutes (Luke 15:30).

2. Music at departure versus music at arrival: Having caught up with Jacob, Laban says he would have wanted to mark Jacob's departure "with mirth and songs, with tambourine and lyre" (Gen. 31:27 ESV). Coming in from the field, the older son hears "music and dancing" (Luke 15:25).

3. The anger of Jacob and the older son:[8] Laban is rightly convinced that one of Jacob's party has stolen something from him but cannot prove it. At this point we read, "Then Jacob became angry" (Gen. 31:36 ESV). Likewise, the older son "was angry and was not willing to go in" (Luke 15:28).

4. Claims of ownership: Jacob's father-in-law claims possession of everything ("All that you see is mine," Gen. 31:43 ESV), but the father says the older son owns it

---

8 Bailey observes how in each case the one getting angry is (at least partly) in the wrong. *Jacob and the Prodigal*, 188.

all: "Child, you are always with me, and all my things are yours" (Luke 15:31).[9]

Again, the storyteller has not merely made connections to Genesis as clever literary allusions. The overlaps in wording and ideas also make a rhetorical point, which is particularly apt for the four groups mentioned in Luke 15:1–2: Jacob, a trickster, gets to keep his wealth gained at Laban's expense, and Laban has to come to terms with God's intention to bless an obviously flawed character. Similarly, tax collectors may have cheated the Pharisees and scribes, but they could still be accepted by God.

Joseph

The next set of echoes we will consider are from the Joseph story (Gen. 37–50). At least one connection is generally recognized, and there is even a cross-reference to it in the widely used academic edition of the Greek New Testament, the Nestle-Aland *Novum Testamentum Graece*, which at Luke 15:22 notes a connection with Genesis 41:42.[10]

Then Pharaoh took his signet *ring* from his hand and put it on Joseph's hand, and clothed him in *garments of fine linen* and put a gold chain about his neck. (Gen. 41:42 ESV)

But the father said to his servants, "Quick! Bring out the *best robe*, and put it on him, and put a *ring* on his hand and shoes on his feet." (Luke 15:22)

9 Noted in Bailey, *Jacob and the Prodigal*, 188–89.
10 Hofius observes the parallel. "Alttestamentliche Motive," 243. See Nestle-Aland, *Novum Testamentum Graece*, 28th ed. (Stuttgart: Deutsche Bibelgesellschaft, 2012).

Both these verses are not just the only two Bible verses referring to the giving of a ring and a special robe but are also the only two stories in the Bible in which someone is transformed instantly and lastingly from rags to riches.[11] It is therefore natural to compare them.

What is more, like the younger son, Joseph is a son who goes off to a far country and whom his father counts as dead yet turns out to be alive.

> And he [Jacob] identified it [Joseph's robe] and said, "It is my son's robe. A fierce animal has devoured him. Joseph is without doubt torn to pieces." (Gen. 37:33 ESV)

> And Israel said, "It is enough; Joseph my son is still alive. I will go and see him before I die." (Gen. 45:28 ESV)

> "For this my son was dead and is alive again; he was lost and is found." (Luke 15:24)

> "But it was necessary to celebrate and be glad, for this your brother was dead and is alive again, and he was lost and is found." (Luke 15:32)

Not only are these two stories the only instances in the Bible of a father considering his son dead and then finding him to be alive

---

11 The story of Mordecai's exaltation in Est. 6 is somewhat different as, at that point, it is only a temporary exaltation. In Est. 8:10 he gets a ring (temporarily), and then in 8:15 as a separate act gets a robe. Daniel is also quickly exalted before Belshazzar but not from a situation of abasement (Dan. 5:29).

again, they also both contain a "severe famine," which is, of course, a major theme of the Joseph story (Gen. 41:31, 56–57; Luke 15:14).

Like Luke 15, the story of Joseph is also about the relationship between brothers and about forgiveness. Joseph has far more reason to be upset with his brothers, who sold him into slavery, than the older son has to be upset with the younger son.

But as with the Jacob-Esau layer and the Jacob-Laban layer, Luke 15 also has reversals relative to the Joseph story:

1. Whereas the younger son finds during the famine that *no one* will give him anything to eat (Luke 15:16), Joseph is the one who supplies *everyone*: "Moreover, all the earth came to Egypt to Joseph to buy grain, because the famine was severe over all the earth" (Gen. 41:57 ESV).
2. Whereas in Luke 15 the father orders the killing of the beast when he sees his son, in Genesis 43:16 it is Joseph who commands this when he sees his younger brother.
3. Whereas in Luke 15 the father supplies clothes for his son, in Genesis 45:22 Joseph supplies clothing to his brothers, who previously took his clothing from him.
4. Whereas in Luke 15 the father rescues his son from poverty, in Genesis 45:11 it is Joseph who rescues his brothers from poverty.

But there are still more echoes of Genesis to consider.

Judah

There is a possible connection between Luke 15 and the gripping story of Judah and Tamar in Genesis 38, which is itself surrounded by the Joseph story. Some people I have shared this with find this parallel less convincing, but I include it here anyway. If you are not persuaded, you can ignore it and still follow the general argument of this book.

In Luke 15 the older son speaks of the *goat* that he wanted to eat with his *friends* and then immediately accuses his brother of devouring his father's livelihood with *prostitutes*.[12] A scribe might well observe that there is only one other place in Scripture where a goat, a friend, and a prostitute come together.

In Genesis there are eleven references to goats but only two texts where prostitutes are mentioned,[13] and in the entire Old Testament, there is only *one* where a goat and a prostitute are mentioned together, namely, the story of Judah and Tamar (Gen. 38:20–22).[14] So when a goat and prostitutes are mentioned in *adjacent verses*, a scribe in the story in Luke 15:29–30 might make a mental connection.

But the older son says he wants to eat a young goat with his *friends*. The Greek word "friend" is *philos* (φίλος), and its most ready Hebrew equivalent is *rea'* (רֵעַ), which occurs seven times in Genesis, five times in the sense of "companion" (Gen. 11:3, 7; 15:10; 31:49; 43:33). The only two occurrences where it means "friend" are in the same story about Judah and Tamar (38:12, 20).

---

12 The accusation may be inspired by Prov. 29:3, "He who loves wisdom makes his father glad, / but a companion of prostitutes squanders his wealth" (ESV).

13 There are several words that are sometimes translated "goat." The most common one, *'ez* (עֵז), occurs eleven times in Genesis (15:9; 27:9, 16; 30:32, 33, 35; 31:38; 32:14; 37:31; 38:17, 20). The word *zonah* (זוֹנָה), "prostitute," occurs only three times (Gen. 34:31; 38:15, 24); a more euphemistic term, *qedeshah* (קְדֵשָׁה), "cult prostitute," is used three times in Gen. 38:21–22.

14 Goat, friends, and a prostitute also all occur in the Samson narratives but not in close proximity.

It is not just that a friend, a goat, and a prostitute occur in the same chapter; they are *in the same short section*, where the friend is trying to deliver a goat as payment for Judah's engagement with the prostitute and thus retrieve the unique personal effects he left with her as pledge of payment for sex. The prostitute, of course, cannot be found because she was not actually a professional prostitute but Judah's daughter-in-law pretending to be a prostitute so that her father-in-law would make her pregnant.

Because Judah had nothing with which to pay the *prostitute* (his daughter-in-law) at the time he engaged her services, he sends his *friend* to give a *goat* as payment and to get back Judah's seal, cord, and staff—the seal in particular would have been a unique identifier of Judah. When the prostitute is not found, Judah tells his friend not to seek further, "or we shall be laughed at" (38:23)—which, ironically enough, is just what happens when Judah's cover-up attempt is recorded in the Bible.

Given that Luke 15 clearly alludes to the Joseph story—the ring, the robe, the great famine, and the son who was dead and alive again—it is striking that these three terms, *friend*, *goat*, and *prostitute*, converge within Genesis 38, which is about Judah, not Joseph. But Genesis 38 is deeply connected to the surrounding chapters about Joseph. After the Joseph story has begun in Genesis 37 and Joseph has been sold into Egypt at the end of that chapter, there is an *interlude* on the activities of Joseph's brother Judah in Genesis 38 before the narrative of Joseph resumes in Genesis 39 and continues through at least Genesis 45. So Joseph is the central figure in Genesis 37–45, except in Genesis 38, where he is not mentioned and Judah and Tamar take center stage.

Thus, an otherwise coherent story appears to be interrupted by something superficially alien.[15]

But Genesis 37, 38, and 39 have close links, even though they feature different characters. Genesis 37 and Genesis 38 are linked by *the identification of a unique personal item*. In Genesis 37, after Joseph's brothers have stripped him of his special robe and sold him into Egypt, they dip the robe in goat's blood to pretend to their father, Jacob, that Joseph is dead. They send (Heb. root *shalakh* / שָׁלַח) the item to Jacob and ask, "Please identify [Heb. root *nakar* / נָכַר] whether it is your son's robe or not" (37:32 ESV). In Genesis 38, after Tamar has become pregnant, Judah, not knowing the child is his, wants Tamar to be burned to death. We then read,

> As she was being brought out, she sent [*shalakh*] word to her father-in-law, "By the man to whom these belong, I am pregnant." And she said, "Please identify [*nakar*] whose these are, the signet and the cord and the staff." Then Judah identified [*nakar*] them and said, "She is more righteous than I." (38:25–26 ESV)

Likewise, Genesis 38 and 39 have links. They contain the sexual encounters of Judah and Joseph, respectively, with women with whom they leave personal items that identify them: Judah leaves his signet, cord, and staff with Tamar, and Joseph leaves his garment as he flees from the advances of Potiphar's wife (39:12). Here the behavior of Judah and Joseph, both away from their family,

---

15 Often the Bible has adjacent narratives that are meant to be compared with each other. As some examples, Gen. 1:1–2:3 parallels 2:4–25; Gen. 4:17–22 parallels 5:1–32; Luke 1:5–25 parallels 1:26–45.

strongly contrasts. Judah engages in sex with Tamar, whom he thinks is a prostitute, whereas Joseph refuses the propositions of Potiphar's wife.

The potential echoes in Luke 15 of the friend, the goat, and the prostitute of the Judah and Tamar story also have moral power. This is because Judah is not merely one of Joseph's eleven brothers but the most prominent one within both the Joseph story and the wider Old Testament.[16] He is the progenitor of David's royal line and the eponym of all the Jews, since the word *Jew* comes from his name. According to biblical tradition, Israel originally consisted of twelve tribes, but ten of these were conquered and exiled around 722 BC, leaving the tribe of Judah as the most prominent remainder, which, despite its own exile to Babylon in 586 BC, came to dominate. In the time of Jesus, there were still Jews who traced their ancestry to other tribes: many Levites traced their ancestry to Levi, Paul traced his ancestry to Benjamin (Phil. 3:5), and the prophetess Anna was from the tribe of Asher (Luke 2:36). Nevertheless, there was a sense in which Judah stood as a preeminent ancestor among the twelve sons of Jacob.

So if Luke 15 reminded Jewish scribes of Genesis 38, it reminded them of the sexual exploits of their own ancestor Judah with someone dressed as a prostitute.

---

16 Sometimes other sons receive individual attention: Reuben (Gen. 37:21–22, 29; 42:22, 37), Simeon (42:24, 36; 43:23), and Benjamin (42:4, 36; 43:14–16, 29, 34; 44:12; 45:12, 14, 22). But Judah has the leading role, coming up with the original idea of selling Joseph (37:26–27), persuading Jacob to let Benjamin travel (43:8), being highlighted as the leader ("When Judah and his brothers came to Joseph's house . . . ," 44:14), and making the longest speech in the Joseph cycle, which provokes Joseph to identify himself (44:18–34). It is Judah alone who offers to take the place of Benjamin as servant to Joseph.

In Luke 15 the older son believes that his brother has squandered his money with prostitutes while in a distant land. Meanwhile, in Genesis the younger brother Joseph, in a distant land and regarded by his father as dead, has actually *resisted* sexual temptation, while his older brother Judah has not.

It is not unlikely that some of the "sinners" mentioned as the audience in Luke 15:1 were prostitutes since in the similar passage in Matthew 21:32, tax collectors and prostitutes are in view. Now if the older son had been wishing that he himself were with prostitutes, and some of the "sinners" mentioned in Luke 15:1 were prostitutes, then the story, read through the lens of Genesis 38–39, undermines the Pharisees' and scribes' neat notions of who is truly virtuous. When Joseph was in a far country, away from the eyes of all his family, he resisted sexual temptation by Potiphar's wife. Meanwhile, Judah the ancestor of the Jews indulged his lusts. Pharisees and scribes despised tax collectors and sinners. But what if the sinners were not quite as sinful as they thought? What if actually the Pharisees' and scribes' own hearts were more enslaved to sin than those they regarded as "sinners"?

In Genesis 38 Judah is ready to have Tamar judged and burned to death, only relenting when she produces evidence that she is in fact pregnant by him (38:24–26). Likewise, the Pharisees and scribes were condemning sinners, including prostitutes, rather as Judah initially does with Tamar. Judah's problem, of course, is that he has been Tamar's "client," and she can prove it.[17]

---

17 It is quite possible that Pharisees were sometimes clients of prostitutes. Though the occasional rabbinic references to rabbis attending prostitutes do not appear as straightforward historical reporting, the very fact that it was discussed reflects a context in which it was at least conceivable. See Babylonian Talmud Avodah Zarah 17a; Hagigah 15a; Qiddushin 81b.

In Genesis righteousness does not lie with the older brother Judah but with the younger brother Joseph. But there is a positive lesson about Judah. Although he initially displays judgmental and hypocritical attitudes toward Tamar, he later appears in a better light, accepts responsibility for his younger brother Benjamin, and is prepared to say to his father that if anything happens to his younger brother, he has sinned before him:

> If I do not bring him [Benjamin] to you and set him before you, then I have sinned before you forever. (43:9; see also 42:21; 44:32)

Compare the words of the younger son to the father: "I have sinned against heaven and before you" (Luke 15:18, 21). Not only is this the only time in Genesis that someone explicitly accepts that he has sinned, but in both Genesis and Luke, *these are the words of a son to his father in relation to the father's youngest boy being lost.*

Judah not only accepts that he is guilty if he has not protected his younger brother, but he is even prepared to offer himself to the vizier of Egypt (his brother Joseph) as a slave. He says to Joseph,

> Now therefore, please let your servant remain instead of the boy as a servant to my lord, and let the boy go back with his brothers. (Gen. 44:33 ESV)

Compare the younger son's words:

> Treat me as one of your hired servants. (Luke 15:19 ESV)

Thus, whereas in Luke 15 the farm-owning older son has not looked after his little brother but resentfully thinks of himself as a slave, in Genesis 44 Judah is willing to take the position of slave for the sake of his younger brother Benjamin. In that sense Judah aligns more with the younger son, who is prepared to be accepted back as a servant.

Listening to Jesus's parable with the story of Judah in the background, the Pharisees and scribes receive a clear moral challenge: (1) Like your ancestor Judah, you are not more innocent than those you condemn. (2) Your ancestor Judah was prepared to accept responsibility before his father for his younger brother—and even to accept slavery to save him. What are you prepared to do for the tax collectors and sinners?

I hope that, so far, you are appreciating the genius of our storyteller, but there is still more to explore as we come to our next layer, which connects the story with Abraham.

Abraham

Isaac had two and only two sons, but famously, Abraham also had two contrasting sons, Ishmael and Isaac, and multiple elements in Luke 15 link with the Abraham story.

1. Abraham is the *archetypal father*—the most famous human father figure in the Old Testament. He gets called Abraham because God promises that he will be "*father* of a multitude of nations" (Gen. 17:5 ESV).[18]
2. Abraham is also the Bible's first *host*, providing a feast, including a calf that would feed hundreds, for three guests

---

18 The *ab-* of Abraham means "father."

(one of whom turns out to be God) at the Bible's first recorded meal, in Genesis 18.[19] As the first man in the Bible to entertain, and as one who entertains God himself, Abraham is later depicted as the one who presides over God's great banquet (see Luke 13:28–29; 16:22).

3. Besides the father in Luke 15, Abraham is the Bible's *only other aged figure who runs*: "He lifted up his eyes and looked, and behold, three men were standing in front of him. When he saw them, he *ran* from the tent door to meet them and bowed himself to the earth" (Gen. 18:2 ESV); "And Abraham *ran* to the herd and took a calf, tender and good" (18:7 ESV). Abraham's running is particularly noteworthy because he seems to have been ninety-nine years old at the time (17:24).

4. Abraham is the *first person in the Bible recorded as running*. A scribe may well notice that this is the first time he has to copy the word "run."

5. In Luke 15:22 the father's first word is "Quick," followed by a string of commands leading to the killing of the fattened calf. Abraham's first word as he begins to prepare for his three guests is also "Quick." In fact, the whole scene is dominated by speed: "And Abraham *went quickly* into the tent to Sarah and said, '*Quick*! Three seahs of fine flour! Knead it, and make cakes.' And Abraham ran to the herd and took a calf, tender and good, and gave it to a young man, who prepared it *quickly*" (Gen. 18:6–7 ESV). Abraham is the first person in the Bible ever to tell

19 This does not count as meals the ill-fated consumption of Gen. 3:6 nor Melchizedek's provision of bread and wine in 14:18.

anyone to hurry, with the first speech beginning with a command to hurry.

6. Abraham is *the only Old Testament person to give away the inheritance while he is still alive.*[20] Genesis 25:5–6 records, "Abraham gave all he had to Isaac. But to the sons of his concubines Abraham gave gifts, and while he was still living he sent them away from his son Isaac, eastward to the east country."

This last connection involves a contrast: whereas the father in Luke 15 divides his wealth between the two sons, Abraham does not. The older son in Luke 15 gets a *better* deal than Abraham's older son Ishmael, who gets no inheritance. The older son therefore has no ground for complaint. This highlights that the Pharisees and scribes have no basis for resenting that Jesus offers tax collectors and sinners a spiritual inheritance. Jesus's story reminds them that Ishmael had far more reason to be upset than they had. He was the son of Hagar, Sarah's servant, and was given no inheritance.

But the narrative of Isaac and Ishmael also raises the question "What is the right response?" Ishmael has to cope with having a younger brother surpass him. Like the father of Luke 15, Abraham throws a feast for his younger son—in this case, when Isaac is weaned:

And the child [Isaac] grew and was weaned. And Abraham made a great feast on the day that Isaac was weaned. But Sarah saw the son of Hagar the Egyptian, whom she had borne to Abraham, laughing. So she said to Abraham, "Cast out this slave woman

20 See Kenneth E. Bailey, *Finding the Lost: Cultural Keys to Luke 15* (St. Louis, MO: Concordia, 1992), 113.

with her son, for the son of this slave woman shall not be heir with my son Isaac." And the thing was very displeasing to Abraham on account of his son. But God said to Abraham, "Be not displeased because of the boy and because of your slave woman. Whatever Sarah says to you, do as she tells you, for through Isaac shall your offspring be named. And I will make a nation of the son of the slave woman also, because he is your offspring." (Gen. 21:8–13 ESV)

This brings us to a final connection:[21] the older son in Jesus's story, like Ishmael, *despises the feast for his younger brother.*

So if the Pharisees and scribes spotted these echoes (which they might well not have done), the story should have challenged them. Did they really want to be like Ishmael? If not, they needed to celebrate the feast for the younger son. They needed to celebrate that tax collectors and sinners were eating with Jesus and wanted to hear his words. In the case of Ishmael, it was his mockery of the feast for Isaac that led to his being cast out and not inheriting (Gen. 21:9–10). Likewise, if the Pharisees and scribes would not accept the tax collectors and sinners who came to Jesus, they would be cast out of their inheritance.

Cain and Abel

For our final biblical layer, we should consider the first brothers in the Bible: Cain and Abel. Though Adam later had other sons

---

21 In addition to the contrast above that Abraham did not divide his inheritance between his two sons, Abraham contrasts with the father in Luke 15 in another way: Abraham would not allow his younger son to go to a far-off country. The longest chapter in Genesis (chap. 24) is all about how Abraham would *not* allow Isaac personally to go away to find a wife but instead sent a servant.

(Gen. 5:3–4), he also famously at one time was a man who had only two sons, like the father of Luke 15:11. Cain and Abel, as well as being the first brothers in the Bible, also illustrate the first case of family conflict. When God accepts Abel and his offering, and not Cain and his offering, Cain, the older brother, is "very angry" (Gen. 4:5). So the Bible's first record of anger is from an older brother envious of the acceptance of his younger brother, just as we have in Luke 15. Both Genesis and Jesus's story associate the older brother with the field (Gen. 4:2, 8; Luke 15:25) and the younger brother with the care of animals (Gen. 4:2; Luke 15:15). In both passages the older brother complains of unfairness (Gen. 4:13–14; Luke 15:29–30). There are also similarities between God and the father figure as they reason with the resentful older brother (Gen. 4:1, 6–7; Luke 15:31–32).[22]

Wider Old Testament Connections

Thus, this short story has abundant connections with major narratives across Genesis: Cain and Abel, Abraham, Isaac and Ishmael, Jacob and Esau, Jacob and Laban, and Joseph and his brothers, especially Judah. Even if some of the connections explored above are explained away as common elements that occur in any story about family dynamics, many connections are striking and cluster together. For Abraham, the sequence of an old man running, then saying "Quick," and then preparing a calf for his

---

22 Tim Keller notes the similarities between the story of Cain and Abel and Luke 15: "Jesus knew the Bible thoroughly, and he knew that at its very beginning it tells another story of an elder and younger brother—Cain and Abel. In that story, God tells the resentful and proud older brother '*You* are your brother's keeper.'" *The Prodigal God: Recovering the Heart of the Christian Faith* (New York: Dutton, 2008), 81.

guests (Gen. 18:2–8) is a clear parallel to the story in Luke 15. The correspondence between the wording of Esau's embrace and kiss of Jacob and the father's welcome of the younger son is again rather precise, as is the correspondence between Jacob's complaint of long work to Laban and the older son's complaint of slaving on the estate to the father. The Joseph story—the son whom the father counts as dead and alive again—is likewise a pattern for the ring and robe for the younger son.

The allusions of Luke 15 to the stories in Genesis vary in how striking they are, but four features should impress us:

1. Some allusions are very specific.
2. There are many allusions.
3. The allusions are particularly concentrated on Genesis and cover the whole book of Genesis.
4. The allusions carry moral challenges exactly suited to an audience of Pharisees and scribes.

I have not mentioned in this book every possible parallel between Genesis and the story of the two sons. But even if I have occasionally seen parallels that are merely coincidental, this does not invalidate my central argument that Jesus's story contains allusions to stories right across Genesis. It is, of course, possible to find parallels between all sorts of texts if you look hard enough, but it is still hard to credit all these parallels merely to hard searching. The text of the story of the two sons is *simply too short* to provide enough material for that.

We can easily list seven features unique to the story of the two sons and the book of Genesis:

1. An old man running
2. A man giving away his inheritance while he is still alive
3. A man saying "Quick" and then making preparations for a feast with a fattened calf
4. A man running, embracing, and kissing
5. A ring and a robe being given, radically changing someone's status
6. A man complaining about how many years he has been working for a father figure
7. The combination of the words *friend*, *goat*, and *prostitute*

But these are merely a selection of parallels. Many of the echoes we have considered are strong but not unique, such as the opening "A (certain) man had two sons." Clearly, this concentration of parallels in a story less than two and a half minutes long cannot be explained merely by the modern interpreter's desire to find similarities.

I have focused on ways that Luke 15:11–32 connects with Genesis but do not want to suggest that it connects only with Genesis. The Nestle-Aland *Novum Testamentum Graece* margin points out connections with six Old Testament passages and with four references from Jewish apocryphal writings.[23] The parallel between the younger son's words "I have sinned against heaven and before you" (Luke 15:18, 21) and Pharaoh's words to Moses and Aaron "I have sinned against the LORD your God, and against you" (Ex. 10:16 ESV) might even incline an attentive scribe to consider the

---

23 The biblical allusions include Gen. 41:42; Ex. 10:16; 2 Sam. 14:33; Ps. 51:6; Prov. 29:3; Dan. 3:5, 10, 15. The apocryphal allusions include Tob. 3:17; 1 Macc. 10:30; 11:9; Ben Sira 33:20–24.

younger son's repentance to be as insincere as Pharaoh's.[24] The combination of the older brother "drawing near," hearing dancing, and getting angry in the context of a celebration involving a calf may remind us of Moses:

And as soon as he *came near* the camp and saw the *calf* and the *dancing*, Moses' *anger burned hot*. (Ex. 32:19 ESV)[25]

In that context Moses is rightly angry at the Israelites' idolatry with the golden calf. In the story of the two sons, the older son, who claims that he has not disobeyed his father's commands, is self-righteously angry. This echo could rather dig at any Pharisee or scribe who sees himself as jealous for rule keeping like Moses. The older son clearly shows that anger at rule breaking can also hide bitterness and a lack of willingness to share resources. The words of the older son "I never disobeyed your command" (Luke 15:29) parallel the confession that a man is supposed to make when tithing and, ironically, when

24 Bailey, *Jacob and the Prodigal*, 106; Hofius, "Alttestamentliche Motive," 241–42. Drury observes parallels to Ex. 10:16; 1 Kings 8:47–49; Prov. 29:3; Hos. 2:7. *Parables in the Gospels*, 145–46. Jeremiah 31:1–22 has a connection with the celebrations as God is seen "far off" (31:3) by wayward Israel, whose watchmen call, "Arise, and let us go" (31:6; cf. Luke 15:18). God is portrayed as "father" (Jer. 31:9) and Israel as "son" (31:20). Israel is explicitly called "Jacob" (31:7, 11). God has mercy (31:20) on his returning child, and the return is celebrated with dance (31:4, 13). In the same context, God is likened to a shepherd (31:10), and a woman, Rachel (31:15), mourns the loss of her children and is told not to mourn because they will return. Bailey maintains that the response of the father to the younger son "while yet at a distance" comes from Isa. 57:19. *Jacob and the Prodigal*, 107.

25 In the Greek translation of the Old Testament, the four key terms of vocabulary— *engizō* (ἐγγίζω), "draw near"; *moschos* (μόσχος), "calf"; *choroi* (χοροί), "dances"; and *orgizomai* (ὀργίζομαι), "be angry"—are identical to those in the parable.

he has ensured that all the needy people who depend on him have been fed (Deut. 26:13).[26]

Rabbinic Echoes

Parables were commonly used among rabbis and have been described as "an almost exclusively Palestinian practice."[27] So Luke 15 reflects not only much of Genesis but also the ways local rabbis of Jesus's time spoke. Rabbinic parables can be hard to date precisely. Many come from around the time of Jesus but are preserved in Jewish literary works centuries later than the New Testament. Since there is no serious likelihood, however, that the Jews who handed down these parables were influenced by the New Testament parables, they are an independent testimony to the way rabbis sometimes taught around the time of Jesus.[28]

There are rabbinic parallels to the two stories of the lost sheep and the lost coin, which immediately precede the story of the two sons in Luke 15.[29] In one parable, it is Moses who rescues a runaway sheep, carrying it on his shoulders, and who, because of this, is appointed to lead (shepherd) Israel.[30] The contrast in the story of the lost sheep between *the ninety-nine* and *the one* also corresponds to a frequent pattern among the rabbis of contrasting

26 Hofius, "Alttestamentliche Motive," 244.

27 Harvey K. McArthur and Robert M. Johnston, *They Also Taught in Parables: Rabbinic Parables from the First Centuries of the Christian Era* (Grand Rapids, MI: Zondervan, 1990), 108.

28 Some of the most relevant parables have been collected in McArthur and Johnston, *They Also Taught in Parables.*

29 There are also rabbinic parallels to the idea of a prodigal son; see, for example, Deuteronomy Rabbah 2.24, in McArthur and Johnston, *They Also Taught in Parables*, 83.

30 Exodus Rabbah 2.2.

the ninety-nine with the one.[31] In another rabbinic parable, the Torah (law) is likened to a lost coin that a man diligently searches for, lighting lamp after lamp.[32] The use of these images in Jesus's stories makes sense if they were already traditional before his time.

If we interpret Jesus's two short stories at the beginning of Luke 15 through the lens of rabbinic parallels, we see again that they make moral points to an audience of Pharisees and scribes. The story of the lost sheep would show the audience the need to imitate Moses *the lawgiver* in caring for the weak and wandering. The story of the lost coin would challenge scribes to search diligently for the law they had lost. These two images are even connected in Luke 15 since it appears that Jesus's opponents had lost sight of the law precisely by neglecting its teaching about how they should treat their neighbors. Jesus appears to be pointing out to the Pharisees and scribes that though they are meant to be experts in God's law, they are missing the recurrent message of Genesis about how God is working in people like the younger son of the story.

Rhetorical Impact

Clearly, all these allusions must come from someone exceedingly well versed both in the Old Testament and in rabbinic discussion. Beyond this, we may say that the presence of the references makes especially good sense *if they were really told by Jesus to exactly the audience described in Luke 15:1–2.* The major echoes of the Genesis stories are not just a vain display of sophistication by a writer composing for a general audience that would in all

31 Mishnah Pe'ah 4.1; Jerusalem Talmud Shabbat 14.3; Bava Metzi'a 107b.
32 Song Rabbah 1.1.9.

likelihood miss them. Rather, they simultaneously present to a biblically literate audience a set of intellectual challenges and, more uncomfortably, a series of moral challenges bound up in the intellectual challenges. Moral challenges to any biblical scholar prepared to reflect on them include the following:

1. Abraham hurries to welcome complete strangers with lavish hospitality.
2. Ishmael loses his inheritance through despising his younger brother.
3. Laban, who loses much of his property to Jacob, has to accept that God wants to bless the man who has taken away his wealth (Gen. 31:24).
4. Esau, who makes bad choices and is tricked out of his inheritance by his younger brother, nevertheless forgives him (Gen. 33:4).
5. Joseph, who is sold by his brothers, forgives them.

All these stories speak into the situation in which the Pharisees and scribes are murmuring about tax collectors and "sinners" approaching Jesus. Abraham, Esau, and Joseph provide positive examples, and Ishmael and Laban offer cautionary cases. Ishmael, Esau, and Laban lose out in property to younger relatives. Pharisees and scribes might think that they will lose out through the hasty inclusion of those they deem unworthy.[33]

The presence of these references, however, must be separated from the question whether Jesus's scribal audience recognized

---

33 "When the father reinstates the younger son, to the diminishment of the older son's share in the estate, the elder brother's heart is laid bare." Keller, *Prodigal God*, 39.

them. Jesus spoke for those with ears to hear and taught in a way that the simple could grasp and the intelligent could miss. It is possible that a biblically literate audience heard the echoes but missed their significance or that they understood their significance but failed to respond. The deeper references are, however, both an invitation and a challenge to experts in Scripture to recognize the knowledge of the storyteller and heed what he says.

3

More Stories Inspired by the Old Testament

SO FAR I HAVE ARGUED that the story of the two sons contains various layers of allusions to the Old Testament. The story was obviously composed by someone who knew the Old Testament well, and it fits exactly with the context claimed in Luke 15:1–2. But if it is true that Jesus told this story with numerous allusions to the Old Testament, we would expect this pattern to be replicated elsewhere in parables attributed to Jesus. This chapter shows that we do indeed find a pattern of Old Testament allusions in other stories and parables of Jesus. These are all shorter than the story of the two sons, and my analysis is likewise much briefer. In this chapter we consider the story of the rich man and Lazarus in more detail and then provide brief notes on the use of the Old Testament in fourteen more stories credited to Jesus in Matthew, Mark, and Luke. Here we begin to see that it is not satisfactory to credit the Old Testament allusions in

Luke 15 to Luke himself. As we proceed, we will also observe evidence that specific parables come from Palestine and note some cases that show a common mind behind more than one story attributed to Jesus.

The Story of the Rich Man and Lazarus

The story of the rich man and Lazarus in Luke 16:19–31 is arguably presented to the same audience as the stories of Luke 15. After 15:1–2 introduces Jesus's mixed audience of tax collectors, sinners, Pharisees, and scribes, 16:1 presents him as addressing just his disciples. Yet the Pharisees are clearly still listening (16:14–15). As a hard-hitting parable against wealthy people who think they can invoke Abraham as their father, the story of the rich man and Lazarus has many thematic and verbal connections both with Luke 15 and the first part of Luke 16 (the parable of the unjust manager), so it is appropriate to see the audience as continuing from Luke 15. Here is the story:

> There was a rich man who used to wear purple and fine linen, celebrating every day in luxury. But a poor man named Lazarus was cast at his gate, covered with sores and longing to be filled with the things that fell from the rich man's table. But even the dogs came and licked his sores. Now it happened that the poor man died and was carried up by the angels to Abraham's side. The rich man also died and was buried. And in Hades he lifted up his eyes, being in torment, and saw Abraham from afar and Lazarus at his side. So he called and said, "Father Abraham, have pity on me, and send Lazarus to dip the tip of his finger in water and cool my tongue because I am in agony in this flame."

But Abraham said, "Child, remember that you received your good things in your lifetime, and Lazarus similarly received bad things, but now he is comforted here and you are in agony. And besides all this, between us and you a great chasm has been fixed, so that those who want to go from here to you cannot, nor can they cross over from there to us." But he said, "I ask you then, father, that you send him to my father's house—for I have five brothers—so that he can testify to them, so that they will not also come to this place of torment." But Abraham said, "They have Moses and the Prophets; let them listen to them." But he said, "No, father Abraham, but if someone from the dead goes to them, they will repent." But he said to him, "If they do not listen to Moses and the Prophets, they will not be persuaded even if someone rises from the dead."

This story shows various connections with the Old Testament. Initially, we are told just two things about the rich man: he wore fabulous clothes, specifically purple and linen, and he feasted luxuriously every day (16:19). Thinking as a scribe who has spent years copying and attending to the exact wording of the Bible, we may note that the only other text that mentions daily feasting with purple and linen together is in the book of Esther, in which Ahasuerus (Xerxes) the Persian king holds a celebration lasting 180 days with a seven-day feast at the end, and it is specifically said that the decor includes purple and linen:

There were white cotton curtains and violet hangings fastened with cords of fine *linen* and *purple* to silver rods and marble pillars, and also couches of gold and silver. (Est. 1:6 ESV)

So the rich man seems to be treating himself like royalty. We see the same pattern of using Scripture here as in Luke 15 because this use also involves *contrast* and *moral challenge*: whereas the Persian king invites great and small to his feast (Est. 1:5), the rich man does not. Lazarus remains outside at the gate, the very place that the book of Esther associates ten times with the hero Mordecai (Est. 2:19, 21; 3:2, 3; 4:2, 6; 5:9, 13; 6:10, 12). Like the parable of the rich man and Lazarus, the book of Esther shows us that it does not end well for the rich man (Haman), who despises the man at the gate, whereas the man at the gate is honored by the king himself and ends up wearing linen and purple (Est. 8:15).

The story of the rich man and Lazarus also links with the only time in the Old Testament when someone has a different feast each day (rather than a continuous multiday feast), namely, the feasts of Job's children:

> His sons used to go and hold a feast in the house of each one on his day, and they would send and invite their three sisters to eat and drink with them. (Job 1:4 ESV)

We note that the word used for the rich man's daily feast is the word "celebrate," which is also used in the story of the two sons both when the father celebrates the return of the younger son and when the older son wishes he could "celebrate" with his friends (Luke 15:24, 29).

With admirable economy of words, the storyteller says that the poor man *is laid* at the gate of the rich man, thus indicating that he is not merely poor but also suffers from a mobility disability.

He has been brought by others to what seems like a strategic spot from which to get help.

The rich man, whose name must have been known to many, is unnamed in the story, whereas Lazarus is named, indicating his greater importance to the storyteller and thus to God himself. We are then informed that Lazarus was covered with sores. Having just evoked the feasting of Job's children, a scribe should know that the only other biblical character covered with sores was Job himself (Job 2:7). In this we see *reversal* relative to the Old Testament, which is characteristic of other stories attributed to Jesus. Job was covered with sores like Lazarus but differed dramatically from him by being wealthy. We also have a moral challenge combined with a reversal since rich Job could claim that he had always helped the poor (Job 31:16–22). Thus, Job was different from the rich man.

We then read that Lazarus was "*longing to be filled* with the things that fell from the rich man's table. But even the dogs came and licked his sores" (Luke 16:21). The wording matches the immediately preceding chapter, in which the younger son "was *longing to be filled* with the pods that the pigs ate, and no one was giving him anything" (15:16). The sequence "longing to be filled" followed by the name of a proverbially unclean animal (pig or dog) shows a link between pigs and dogs similar to the one we see on Jesus's lips exclusively in Matthew's Gospel:

> Do not give dogs what is holy, and do not throw your pearls before pigs, lest they trample them underfoot and turn to attack you. (Matt. 7:6 ESV)

Since these parallels between pigs and dogs are attributed to Jesus in completely different contexts in two different Gospels, it makes most sense if they go back to Jesus himself.

In the story, the poor man dies first, as poor people typically do. Nothing is noted about his burial, and we are thus left wondering whether he is actually buried. Then the rich man dies, and his burial is noted (Luke 16:22). But whereas the rich man's death is publicly marked, it is the poor man who receives VIP treatment and is carried by angels to Abraham's side, or what older English translations call "Abraham's bosom."

Since there is no reason to suppose that Abraham in his post-mortem existence has anything other than a normal-sized body, we must assume that his side is where the most privileged person is placed in the heavenly feast, not a superlarge heavenly area where many people could fit.[1] The word "side," or "bosom," expresses where a close dining companion might lean (see John 1:18; 13:23). Thus, in line with Jesus's saying that the first will be last and the last first, Lazarus, who is last in this life, gets the top place at the heavenly feast at which Abraham presides (Luke 13:28–30).

The rich man, meanwhile, is in Hades—a word that does not here convey all the complex geography of Greek mythology but does at least designate a place where people are paid back for what they have done in this life. Just as Lazarus's sores had burned him and had been licked by the tongues of dogs, so now the rich man's tongue is on fire, and he yearns for relief.

---

1   In the book of Jubilees, a piece of apocryphal literature probably well known at the time of Jesus, the "bosom" of Abraham was clearly a normal physical space since it is where the young Jacob slept when Abraham died (Jub. 23).

Then the story says that the rich man "lifted up his eyes, being in torment, and saw Abraham from afar" (Luke 16:23). For Bible experts, there are only two places in the Old Testament where the combination of "lift up eyes" and "from afar" occurs, both in stories about rich men. The first is about Abraham and the second about Job:

On the third day Abraham lifted up his eyes and saw the place from afar. (Gen. 22:4 ESV)

And when they [Job's three friends] lifted up their eyes from afar, they did not recognize him [Job]. And they lifted up their voices and wept. (Job 2:12)

We have already been contextually reminded of Job by the daily feasting and the body covered with sores. We here have the combination of lifting up the eyes and seeing a particular person from afar. Even Job's rather useless friends are moved with compassion when they see Job covered with sores. At least they try to help since they travel considerable distances to see Job. This echo makes a moral point by highlighting how the rich man had done absolutely nothing when he saw Lazarus up close daily, covered with sores.

But the story here has an even closer connection to the account of Abraham, with which it shares four features: "lift up," "eyes," "saw from afar," and Abraham himself. The connection with Abraham is reinforced because he is the Old Testament character who is most often said to lift up his eyes (Gen. 18:2; 22:4, 13).[2] The connection

2   The expression is used once each for Lot, Isaac, Jacob, Esau, and Joseph (Gen. 13:10; 24:63; 33:1, 5; 43:29), only counting instances of third-person masculine singular

with Abraham also makes a moral point: Abraham, like Job, was rich. Job had always helped the poor, and Abraham was hospitable to strangers. But the rich man had done neither.

The rich man now addresses Abraham three times as "Father" (Luke 16:24, 27, 30), just as three times in the previous chapter the younger son had mentally or actually addressed his father as "Father" (15:12, 18, 21). The rich man in addressing Abraham as his father wants to stress his close connection with Abraham. He also reveals in his address to Abraham that, despite having ignored him daily, he knew Lazarus's name:

> Father Abraham, have pity on me, and send Lazarus to dip the tip of his finger in water and cool my tongue because I am in agony in this flame. (16:24)

Just as the father of Luke 15 addressed the older son as "child," so we find that Abraham addresses the rich man as "child" (15:31; 16:25). We will see later that this fits a pattern of evidence pointing to a common mind behind the two stories.[3]

The rich man pleads with Abraham that he would send Lazarus to warn his "five brothers." Why five? One reason more obvious to scribes that the storyteller would use the number *five* here is that there were *five books* of the law of Moses. Say the number "five" to a scribe, and it is hard for him not to think about his

---

verbs in the past tense. Whereas there are eight of these in Genesis, there are only six other instances in the rest of the Old Testament (Num. 24:2; Josh. 5:13; Judg. 19:17; 2 Sam. 18:24; 1 Chron. 21:16; Ezek. 18:12). The case of Job 2:12 is counted separately here because it has a plural verb.

3 See table 2, p. 90.

main job of copying out five particular books. This is not to say that the five brothers in the story stand for the five books of the law. It is rather that the number five may mentally trigger among scribes thoughts of the five books of the law. Further evidence that this link is not alien to the context is that according to Luke 16:16–17, Jesus has explicitly mentioned the law of Moses *in two of the three verses that immediately precede this story*. In 16:17 he even refers to the small pen strokes that scribes had to make on many letters as they copied the law. And in Abraham's response to the rich man, he mentions Moses as a stand-in for the Pentateuch twice, further supporting the link (16:29, 31).

Now let us consider the rich man's statement that he has "five brothers" while thinking at the same time of the five books of the law. In doing so, we realize that the rich man has made a mathematical mistake. If Abraham really is his father, he does not have only five brothers. After all, in the law God promised to Abraham that his descendants would be uncountable, like the stars and like the sand (Gen. 22:17). It therefore follows that if the rich man really is a child of Abraham, he must have vast numbers of brothers. Most awkwardly, Lazarus would be his brother too. Sadly, this man has been ignoring the five books of the law and so has missed this basic fact. The older son had wanted a feast without his father. Similarly, in his own lifetime the rich man had feasts excluding Lazarus, who would have been his brother if he could truly claim that Abraham was his father.

The older son and the rich man have in common that they want to reject as brother someone accepted by that brother's father. This packs a rhetorical punch for an audience of Pharisees and scribes who likewise do not relish the prospect of accepting tax collectors and "sinners" as their own spiritual family yet want to claim God as their Father.

Thus we have another story attributed to Jesus that is powerful at the surface level even if one does not notice any of the echoes to earlier parts of the Bible. But especially for the learned hearer, it also works at a deeper level through a range of clever references to the Jewish Scriptures. The combination of simplicity and depth makes it a work of great artistry and genius.

Fourteen Other Stories

So far, our examples of deep knowledge of the Old Testament have both come from Luke's Gospel. Here I provide briefer notes on fourteen more parables showing that use of the Old Testament in parables is a phenomenon found in Matthew, Mark, and Luke.

1. *The parable of the wise and foolish builders* (Matt. 7:24–27; Luke 6:47–49) occurs in Matthew immediately after a warning against false prophets (Matt. 7:15–20) and echoes Ezekiel 13, which speaks against false prophets, likening them to bad builders whose work is undone by a rainstorm, resulting in a collapse (Ezek. 13:5, 10, 11, 12).

2. *The parable of the strong man* (Matt. 12:29; Mark 3:27; Luke 11:21–22) is about not being able to enter a strong man's house and plunder it unless the strong man is first bound. It echoes a text in Isaiah:

Can the prey be taken from the mighty,
    or the captives of a tyrant be rescued?

For thus says the LORD:

"Even the captives of the mighty shall be taken
   and the prey of the tyrant be rescued,
for I will contend with those who contend with you,
   and I will save your children." (Isa. 49:24–25 ESV)

3. *The parable of the sower* (Matt. 13:3–9; Mark 4:3–9; Luke 8:5–8) describes a man sowing seed on four sorts of ground (by the path, on stony ground, among thorns, in good ground). This contrasts with the command in Jeremiah 4:3: "Do not sow among thorns."[4] The hundredfold fruit borne in the good ground echoes the hundredfold harvest achieved by Isaac in Genesis 26:12.[5]

4. *The parable of the tares* (Matt. 13:24–30) tells of tares growing up, surprisingly, among the wheat. It is reminiscent of Old Testament texts in which good is planted, even by God himself, but bad is harvested:

He looked for it to yield grapes,
   but it yielded wild grapes. (Isa. 5:2 ESV)

Yet I planted you a choice vine,
   wholly of pure seed.

---

4   John Drury, *The Parables in the Gospels: History and Allegory* (London: SPCK, 1985), 52.

5   Harvey K. McArthur and Robert M. Johnston note that Isaac's hundredfold harvest is commented on within a rabbinic parable in Sifre Deut. 8. *They Also Taught in Parables: Rabbinic Parables from the First Centuries of the Christian Era* (Grand Rapids, MI: Zondervan, 1990), 67.

How then have you turned degenerate
    and become a wild vine? (Jer. 2:21 ESV)

They have sown wheat and have reaped thorns.
    (Jer. 12:13 ESV; see also Job 31:40)

As in Joel 3:13, God's coming judgment is likened to a harvest.

5. *The parable of the leaven* (Matt. 13:33; Luke 13:20–21) is arguably Jesus's shortest parable and therefore makes a good contrast with the parable of the two sons, which is his longest story. It is only nineteen words in Matthew and fifteen in Luke in the Greek:

The kingdom of heaven is like leaven that a woman took and hid in *three seahs of flour*, till it was all leavened. (Matt. 13:33)

[The kingdom of God] is like leaven that a woman took and hid in *three seahs of flour*, until it was all leavened. (Luke 13:20–21)

Despite its brevity, this parable appears to come from Palestine not merely because it is a parable—and parables are particularly associated with Palestine—but also because it uses the local Palestinian measure the *seah*.[6]

---

6 Dry measures differed from country to country within the Roman Empire: in Egypt the main dry measure was the *artaba*; in Italy it was the *modius*. The Jewish historian Josephus even needed to explain to his audience what a *seah* was, saying, "A *seah* is equivalent to one and a half Italian modius." Josephus, *Jewish Antiquities* 9.85.

This tiny parable also echoes Abraham's words from a passage we have already considered:

> And Abraham went quickly into the tent to Sarah and said, "Quick! *Three seahs of fine flour*! Knead it, and make cakes." (Gen. 18:6 ESV)

It is connected with Genesis 18:6 not only by the word *seah* but also by the *number of seahs*. The word *seah* (Heb. סְאָה) occurs only nine times in the Old Testament, and Genesis 18:6 is the first occurrence of this word and the only time that it occurs with the number three.[7] In Genesis 18:6 and in Jesus's parable of Matthew 13:33 and Luke 13:21, not only are these the only times when "three seahs" occur, but also the "three seahs" are used as a measure of the same substance—flour—not parched grain, barley, or area, as in other occurrences of the term.

Our study of the story of the two sons has revealed a focus on Genesis 18:6.[8] There the first word from Abraham's mouth is "Quick" (like the father in Luke 15:22), which, like the occurrence here, leads to preparation of a fattened calf to eat. We have also already seen links between Abraham and Luke 15. So both the longest story attributed to Jesus and the shortest story arguably allude to the same verse (Gen. 18:6), which is surely good evidence

---

7 The other occurrences are "*five* seahs of parched grain" brought by Abigail as a gift to David (1 Sam. 25:18), "*two* seahs of seed" used as the measure of the size of the trench Elijah had built around the altar on Mount Carmel (1 Kings 18:32), and the *one* seah of fine flour that Elisha said would be sold for a shekel and *two* seahs of barley that would be sold for a shekel in the gate of Samaria (2 Kings 7:1, 16, 18).

8 See p. 56.

that they come from *the same mind*. This is explained with the utmost simplicity once we accept that Jesus is the source of both.

6. *The parable of the dragnet* (Matt. 13:47–50) compares the kingdom of heaven to a dragnet catching all sorts of fish and then describes the process of sorting the fish into good and bad ones on the beach. This parable fits beautifully with the context of Galilean fishing,[9] but also the fish here clearly stand for people—a connection Jesus makes elsewhere when he calls his disciples to be "fishers of men" (Matt. 4:19; Mark 1:17). The idea of humans being like fish caught in a dragnet is already in Habakkuk 1:14–15:

> You make mankind like the fish of the sea,
>> like crawling things that have no ruler.
> He brings all of them up with a hook;
>> he drags them out with his net;
> he gathers them in his dragnet;
>> so he rejoices and is glad. (ESV)

Jesus explains the parable in language reminiscent of Nebuchadnezzar's fiery furnace in Daniel 3:6:[10]

---

9 Mendel Nun, "The Kingdom of Heaven Is Like a Seine," *Torah Class*, Seed of Abraham Ministries, accessed November 30, 2022, https://torahclass.com/.

10 There are two related early Greek versions of Daniel, both of which appear to be pre-Christian, one preserved in Codex Chisianus 45 (eleventh century, Vatican Library Chig.R.VII.45) and the other in Codex Vaticanus (fourth century) and Codex Alexandrinus (fifth century). In Dan. 3:6 and elsewhere, both translate "into the fiery furnace" as *eis tēn kaminon tou pyros* (εἰς τὴν κάμινον τοῦ πυρός), the exact phrase found in Matt. 13:50.

And whoever does not fall down and worship shall immediately be cast into a burning fiery furnace. (Dan. 3:6 ESV)

So it will be at the end of the age. The angels will come out and separate the evil from the righteous and throw them into the fiery furnace. (Matt. 13:49–50 ESV)

7. *The parable of the lost sheep* (Matt. 18:12–14; Luke 15:4–6) occurs in two different contexts and two slightly different forms. It appears in Luke as the first of a triad leading to the story of the two sons and in Matthew in the context of Jesus's teaching on forgiveness. Related shepherding language with Jesus cast as the shepherd occurs in John 10:1–18. In the Old Testament, God is often likened to a shepherd (e.g., Ps. 23:1–2; Isa. 40:11; Mic. 2:12) and God's people to wandering sheep (e.g., Ps. 119:176; Isa. 53:6). God is specifically portrayed as the one who seeks the lost sheep in Ezekiel 34:6, 12, and 16. The fact that another parable attributed to Jesus has a much clearer reference to Ezekiel 34 makes it more likely that this parable refers to it as well.[11]

8. *The parable of the unforgiving servant* (Matt. 18:23–35) describes a servant who owes the vast sum of ten thousand talents to his king. The number has not been chosen at random but is the exact debt incurred by the servant Haman toward his king, Ahasuerus (Xerxes), in Esther 3:9 and then forgiven by the king in 3:11. The story of the book of Esther involves Haman as senior servant bearing a grudge against Esther's uncle Mordecai. Like

---

11 See on Matt. 25:31–46 below (p. 84).

the unforgiving servant in Jesus's parable, Haman also *falls* (Est. 7:8; cf. Matt. 18:26) when begging to be treated with mercy and is justly punished with the punishment he intended for his social inferior. The use of a number from the Old Testament in this parable is also something we noted for the three seahs of leaven in the parable of the leaven and for the hundredfold increase in the parable of the sower. The reuse of numbers from the Old Testament is easily explained if all these parables are products of the same mind.

9. *The parable of the tenants* (Matt. 21:33–41; Mark 12:1–9; Luke 20:9–16) takes language from many parts of the Old Testament, especially the Song of the Vineyard (Isa. 5:1–7). Both passages concern vineyards and the similar preparations by their owners:

> He dug it and cleared it of stones,
>> and planted it with choice vines;
> he built a watchtower in the midst of it
>> and hewed out a wine vat in it. (Isa. 5:2 ESV)

> There was a master of a house who planted a vineyard and put a fence around it and dug a winepress in it and built a tower. (Matt. 21:33 ESV)

In Isaiah God plants the vineyard, which is Israel. Likewise, in Jesus's parable the vineyard seems to stand for Israel. In the parable the owner repeatedly sends servants who are then ill-treated in language reminiscent of Israel's rejection of the prophets in the Old Testament (e.g., 2 Chron. 24:19, 20–22; 36:15–16; Neh. 9:26; Jer. 7:25–26; 20:2; 25:4; 26:21–23). In response to the rejection of his servants, the owner decides to send his "beloved son" (Mark 12:6; Luke 20:13),[12] an expression that stems from Genesis 22:2, the famous passage about Abraham being commanded to offer up his son Isaac as a sacrifice. On seeing the beloved son, the vineyard tenants react rather like Joseph's brothers did when they saw their brother, who was their father's favorite son:

> They said to one another, "Here comes this dreamer. Come now, let us kill him and throw him into one of the pits." (Gen. 37:19–20 ESV)

> But when the tenants saw the son, they said to themselves, "This is the heir. Come, let us kill him and have his inheritance." And they took him and threw him out of the vineyard and killed him. (Matt. 21:38–39 ESV; cf. Mark 12:7–8; Luke 20:14–15)

The story ends with a quotation from Psalm 118:22–23 (Matt. 21:42; Mark 12:10–11; Luke 20:17 [quoting only Ps. 118:22]).

10. *The parable of the ten virgins* (Matt. 25:1–13) tells of five wise and five foolish virgins. The former have enough oil for their lamps, but the latter do not and so miss the arrival of the bridegroom. Hearers are reminded of Proverbs 13:9 (see also Job 18:5):

---

12 Matt. 21:37 has simply "son," lacking "beloved."

The light of the righteous will rejoice,
    but the lamp of the wicked will go out.

We read that "in the middle of the night a cry went up" (Matt. 25:6). This is the cry that the bridegroom has arrived. It seems an unlikely time for a bridegroom to come, but as John Drury notes, the story of the ten virgins fits exactly with the tenth plague in Egypt, when a cry goes up at midnight (Ex. 12:29–30).[13]

In the tenth plague, there is a sharp division between the fates of two groups, as there is in the story of the ten virgins. Also, during the tenth plague the Israelites are supposed to be eating the Passover lamb in a state of extreme readiness (Ex. 12:11), and similarly, it is for their lack of readiness that the foolish virgins are shut out. In its setting in Matthew, the parable is being told at Passover time, when everyone is being reminded of the Passover story with its cry at midnight. In Matthew as in Luke 15:1–2, the historical setting, if taken seriously, explains why the specific biblical references are used.

11. *The parable of the sheep and the goats* (Matt. 25:31–46) echoes but differs from Ezekiel 34:17: "As for you, my flock, thus says the Lord GOD: Behold, I judge between sheep and sheep, between rams and male goats" (ESV).

12. *The parable of putting the hand to the plow* (Luke 9:61–62) is hard to read without thinking of Elisha in 1 Kings 19:19–21,

13 Drury, *Parables in the Gospels*, 103.

who was plowing but, in contrast to the man in Luke 9:61, was allowed to say farewell to his father and mother.[14]

13. *The parable of the good Samaritan* (Luke 10:25–37) is recorded as Jesus's response to a Jewish legal expert. Thus, as with the story of the two sons, the addressee can be expected to know the Scriptures. The legal expert tests Jesus with the question "Teacher, what must I do to inherit eternal life?" Jesus replies, "In the law, what is written? How do you read it?" To this the man replies, "You shall love the Lord your God with all your heart and with all your soul and with all your strength and with all your understanding, and your neighbor as yourself." In the context this is a model answer, in fact one that in Matthew and Mark Jesus himself gives in answer to the question of what the greatest commandment is (Matt. 22:35–40; Mark 12:28–31).

Jesus replies to the legal expert, "You have answered correctly. This do, and you will live" (Luke 10:28). Hidden in these words is a scriptural knowledge test. Can the legal expert remember the only place in the Bible where we have the sequence (with pronoun preceding imperative) "This do, and you will live"? It is in Genesis 42:18, where Joseph says these words to his brothers, who on their last encounter many years earlier had stripped him and abandoned him naked, just like the man in the parable Jesus is about to tell.[15] This subtle test once again fits the pattern of Jesus demonstrating mastery of the Hebrew Scriptures.

There then follows the parable of the good Samaritan—a story that throughout history has powerfully challenged people to show

---

14 See Kenneth E. Bailey, *Through Peasant Eyes* (Grand Rapids, MI: Eerdmans, 1980), 27.
15 Bailey, *Through Peasant Eyes*, 38.

love across tribal boundaries. The story, which must go back to someone who knew Palestinian geography well,[16] also echoes a relatively obscure Old Testament passage, in which, as in Jesus's story, people from Samaria help naked people from Judah, treating them with oil, putting them on their donkeys, and taking them to Jericho:[17]

> And the men who have been mentioned by name rose and took the captives, and with the spoil they clothed all who were naked among them. They clothed them, gave them sandals, provided them with food and drink, and anointed them, and carrying all the feeble among them on donkeys, they brought them to their kinsfolk at Jericho, the city of palm trees. Then they returned to Samaria. (2 Chron. 28:15 ESV)

When Joseph was naked, his brothers did not help him. So the last time in the Bible someone said, "This do and you will live," was when the victim addressed the guilty and told them of a way to live. Jesus's hidden test to the legal expert is whether he can make the connection and recognize that he is being addressed as one who is guilty. The fact that both the story of the good Samaritan

16 It talks of a man "going down" from Jerusalem to Jericho. The choice of the expression "going down" is significant and shows local knowledge since Jerusalem is about 2,500 feet above sea level and Jericho is about 850 feet below sea level. The road from Jerusalem to Jericho was the main eastward route from Jerusalem and was a perilous road since brigands could easily hide along the way. In the story a priest and a Levite are traveling from Jerusalem, where there was ritual work to do, to Jericho, where many priests lived, as we know from outside the Bible. See Joshua Schwartz, "On Priests and Jericho in the Second Temple Period," *Jewish Quarterly Review* 79, no. 1 (1988): 23–48.

17 This link is noted often; see, for example, Drury, *Parables in the Gospels*, 134.

and the story of the two sons (Luke 15:11–32) connect with the Joseph story to point out the sin of the audience reinforces the impression that they come from the same mind.

14. *The parable of the rich fool* (Luke 12:16–21) reminds us of the story in 1 Samuel 25 of Nabal (whose name means "fool," 25:25), the man who keeps his wealth for his own feasting while spurning David. Nabal then suddenly dies. In Jesus's parable the rich fool's soliloquy encouraging himself to "eat, drink and be merry" right before he suddenly dies is based on Isaiah 22:13, where those who reject God say,

> Let us eat and drink,
>   for tomorrow we die.

The fool quotes the first part but, to his own downfall, forgets how the quotation ends.[18]

Scripture in the Parables

Not every parable attributed to Jesus has clear Old Testament allusions, but such allusions are a common feature of Gospel parables, not merely of those found in Luke's Gospel. It does not explain enough merely to attribute Old Testament allusions in Luke 15:11–32 to Luke the author. The most natural thing is to suppose that Old Testament references go back before the written Gospels to Jesus, the teacher whose words they claim to report.

---

18 Three verses earlier in Isaiah, the people are tearing down existing buildings to make fortifications (Isa. 22:10). The parable may also possibly echo Pss. 39:4–6; 49:16–20; Jer. 17:11.

Someone might object that these Old Testament references could go back before the Gospels and yet still not go all the way back to Jesus. Could not someone else have told stories with significant Old Testament inspiration? Of course, it is possible. But is it likely? Consideration of rabbinic parables suggests not.

Harvey McArthur and Robert Johnston, in their study of rabbinic parables, show copious use of Scripture at the end of parables in the section discussing what is being illustrated but "negligible evidence of the introduction of Scripture into the story half of the rabbinic parables."[19] This supports the view that when we see significant use of the Old Testament in the Gospel parables themselves, we are dealing with a distinguishing trait of a particular teacher, one with extensive knowledge of the Scriptures. Not only are an unusual number of parables attributed to Jesus, but also they often bear the distinctive trait of deep use of Scripture in the details of the story. In the next chapter we consider further evidence that these parables do indeed come from Jesus.

---

19 McArthur and Johnston, *They Also Taught in Parables*, 151.

4

Was Jesus the Genius?

WE HAVE SEEN SO FAR that echoes of the Old Testament are a feature of many parables or stories attributed to Jesus. We have seen numerous Old Testament echoes in the story of the two sons (Luke 15:11–32) and have also seen quite a few in the story of the rich man and Lazarus (Luke 16:19–31). Both stories are well explained and gain rhetorical force if they were actually told to the audience recorded in Luke 15:1–2. We can further observe that these stories have close links with the story placed between them, namely, the parable of the unjust manager (Luke 16:1–9). Table 2 (next page) shows that these three stories are linked by at least twelve key features.

The links are varied. They include opening lines, such as "There was a rich man" (16:1, 19); compositional features, such as a self-address by the protagonist; and central elements, such as the hunger of both the younger son and Lazarus, who were "longing to be filled" (15:16; 16:21). There are artful connections, such as the use of "quickly" with the imperative by both the father and the unjust manager (15:22; 16:6). There are also connections of Old Testament reference since in both stories the "seeing" from "far off" is explicitly or implicitly a reminder of Abraham. As noted earlier, the rich man claims Abraham as his father but refuses to recognize that this would entail the conclusion that Lazarus is his brother. Likewise, the older son denies any relationship with his brother when he says, "this son of yours" (15:30). The combination of the various types of connection suggests that *all three stories come from a single mind*.

Table 2 Links across the Stories in Luke 15:11–16:31

	Two Sons (Luke 15:11–32)	Unjust Manager (Luke 16:1–9)	Rich Man and Lazarus (Luke 16:19–31)
Use of address "Father" three times	15:12, 18, 21	—	16:24, 27, 30
Character introduced as "wasting" possessions, Gk. *diaskorpizō* (διασκορπίζω)	15:13	16:1	—
Character "longing to be filled," Gk. *epithymeō* (ἐπιθυμέω) and *chortasthēnai* (χορτασθῆναι), followed immediately by mention of an unclean animal (pigs or dogs)	15:16	—	16:21
Character asking "how many" or "how much," Gk. words beginning with *pos-* (ποσ-) and distinguished only by their grammatical ending	15:17	16:5, 7	—

(Table 2 continued)

	Two Sons (Luke 15:11–32)	Unjust Manager (Luke 16:1–9)	Rich Man and Lazarus (Luke 16:19–31)
Character addressing himself regarding future action	15:17–19	16:3–4	—
Use of "far off" plus the verb "see"—in one case a father seeing and in the other a father being seen	15:20	—	16:23
Character giving a command to do something "quick(ly)"	15:22	16:6	—
Use of "celebrate," Gk. euphrainomai (εὐφραίνομαι)	15:24, 29, 32	—	16:19
Character described as "calling one" of a group, Gk. proskalesamenos hena (προσκαλεσάμενος ἕνα)	15:26	16:5	—
"Friends," Gk. philoi (φίλοι)	15:29	16:9	—
Character in the wrong addressed as "child," Gk. teknon (τέκνον), by the story's father figure	15:31	—	16:25
Story beginning "There was a rich man," Gk. anthrōpos [. . .] tis ēn plousios (ἄνθρωπος [. . .] τις ἦν πλούσιος)	—	16:1	16:19

Could that mind be the mind of Luke? That would explain why the themes of these stories fit incredibly well with the themes of Luke's Gospel as a whole, particularly the emphasis on including sinners and the poor and excluding the self-righteous and the rich (e.g., 1:53; 6:24–25). It is precisely the convergence of these overarching themes of Luke and the story of the two sons that leads John Drury to think that the author of the Gospel and the originator of the story must be the same person.[1]

Taking Luke to be the inventor of the story of the two sons, however, would not explain why parables recorded only in Matthew also show heavy dependence on the Old Testament. Nor would it explain the fact that the author of the story seems to have come from Palestine.

An Author from the Land of Jesus

Not only are parables particularly characteristic of Palestinian rabbis, but the parable of the unjust manager includes a series of features that are also clearly from Palestine. Here is the parable:

> He also said to the disciples, "There was a rich man who had a manager, and charges were brought to him that this man was wasting his possessions. And he called him and said to him, 'What is this that I hear about you? Turn in the account of your management, for you can no longer be manager.' And the manager said to himself, 'What shall I do, since my master is taking the management away from me? I am not strong enough to dig, and I am ashamed to beg. I have decided what to do, so that when I am removed from management, people

1 John Drury, *The Parables in the Gospels: History and Allegory* (London: SPCK, 1985), 142.

may receive me into their houses.' So, summoning his master's debtors one by one, he said to the first, 'How much do you owe my master?' He said, 'A hundred *baths* [Gk. *batos*, βάτος] of oil.' He said to him, 'Take your bill, and sit down quickly and write fifty.' Then he said to another, 'And how much do you owe?' He said, 'A hundred *cors* [Gk. *koros*, κόρος] of wheat.' He said to him, 'Take your bill, and write eighty.' The master commended the dishonest manager for his shrewdness. For the sons of this world are more shrewd in dealing with their own generation than the *sons of light*. And I tell you, make friends for yourselves by means of *mammon* [Gk. *mamōnas*, μαμωνᾶς] *of unrighteousness*, so that when it fails they may receive you into the eternal dwellings. (Luke 16:1–9 ESV adapted)

The italicized words all represent particularly Palestinian features. The *bath* and the *cor* are, respectively, liquid and dry measures, used in the Old Testament and in Palestine but not elsewhere. The parable then talks about the "sons of light" as a category for the people on God's side, a phrase known from the Dead Sea Scrolls, where a major work was called *The War of the Sons of Light against the Sons of Darkness*. The parable ends by speaking of "mammon of unrighteousness," using the Jewish Aramaic word *mamona'* (ממונא) transcribed into Greek as the word for money. The phrase is also very like the phrase *hon harish'ah* (הון הרשעה), "wealth of unrighteousness," which is found in the Dead Sea Scrolls.[2] Thus, this story has strong links with both economic and religious Jewish vocabulary from Palestine.

2 Cairo Damascus Document 6.15.

It also has a feature we have seen in other stories of Jesus. We have observed that numbers in Jesus's stories often come from the Old Testament. The "three seahs" of Matthew 13:33 were inspired by the same number in Genesis 18:6, the hundredfold growth in Matthew 13:8 was inspired by Isaac's harvest in Genesis 26:12, and the ten thousand talents owed in Matthew 18:24 were inspired by the ten thousand talents owed in Esther 3:9. So likewise, the "hundred baths of oil" in Luke 16:6 and "hundred cors of wheat" in Luke 16:7 seem to come from Ezra 7:22, where the exact same quantities of the same substances occur. Both in Luke and Ezra, these are amounts *owed* to someone—the unjust manager and Ezra, respectively—who is managing affairs on behalf of a higher master.

Since the parable of the unjust manager stands between Jesus's story of the two sons and his story of the rich man and Lazarus and has numerous connections with them, it suggests that all three come from *the same mind*. Since the story of the two sons itself shares deep connections with the story of the lost sheep and the story of the lost coin, both of which share rabbinic echoes, it seems that *all five stories* in Luke 15–16 connect with each other in a complex web of relationships that suggests they come from a single author.

That author must be a brilliant storyteller, able to craft multiple powerful stories and also able to speak to more than one audience at a time. The author also must be deeply familiar with (1) Palestine, (2) the Old Testament, and (3) rabbinic ways of talking. Jesus of Nazareth, the most famous Jewish teacher of all time, fits just this profile.

By contrast, Luke does not fit this profile. He is traditionally thought to have been a Greek from Antioch in Syria. Colossians

4:10–14 seems to imply that he was not a Jew. He was certainly intelligent and carried out thorough research. He was the author not only of the Gospel that bears his name but also of the Acts of the Apostles, which shows considerable familiarity with many places around the Mediterranean. I am certainly not wanting to suggest that he was incapable of telling a good story. But he is not a natural candidate for the author of the specifically Palestinian details of the parable of the unjust manager, nor for the knowledge of rabbinic ideas revealed in Luke 15. What is more, even in the unlikely scenario that a Gospel writer was a much better storyteller than the teacher he credited his stories to, the Gospel writer would have had no reason to put in such a wealth of references to Genesis into such a short story unless he had an audience of Bible scholars in mind. Overall, supposing Luke to be the author of the story of the two sons explains little, while supposing Jesus to be the author explains exactly what we see.

Six Hallmarks of Jesus in Luke 15

In addition to the various reasons we have already seen for attributing the brilliant stories of Luke 15 to Jesus, six more features show a *common mind* behind Luke 15 and what is attributed to Jesus elsewhere, especially in Matthew's Gospel.

Questions Beginning Parables

Matthew and Luke show Jesus opening parables with the same sort of question. Sometimes they have the same wording before the same parable, and at other times they have the same sort of question, but what follows is different. This pattern is best explained if these questions were a feature of Jesus's teaching on multiple occasions. Thus the question at the beginning of Luke 15:4—"What man among you . . . ?"—fits a pattern of Jesus's speech since this is a way of speaking that is attributed to Jesus on seven other occasions in Luke:[3]

Which of you will have a friend . . . ? (Luke 11:5)

Which father among you will his son ask for a fish . . . ? (Luke 11:11 // Matt. 7:9–10)

Which of you by worrying can add . . . ? (Luke 12:25 // Matt. 6:27)

Of which of you will a son or bull fall into a well . . . ? (Luke 14:5 // Matt. 12:11)

For which of you, wanting to build a tower . . . ? (Luke 14:28)

Or what king, going to meet another king in war . . . ? (Luke 14:31)

Which of you, having a slave . . . ? (Luke 17:7)

Since three of these have direct parallels in Matthew, it is not easy to attribute them only to Luke.[4] Even at its best, attributing

3   My argument here is based on Kenneth E. Bailey, *Poet and Peasant: A Literary-Cultural Approach to the Parables in Luke* (Grand Rapids, MI: Eerdmans, 1976), 120–21.

4   The view that the questions in Matthew have arisen through Matthew copying Luke runs into problems. Just to give one instance, there is no straightforward

such common elements between two Gospels to the use of one Gospel by another explains only a portion of the data. An easier explanation is that both Gospels were drawing on a common well—be it memory or written sources—that reported Jesus as speaking this way.

We see further evidence of questions at the beginning of Jesus's parables. The lesser-known story of the two sons (Matt. 21:28–32) also begins with a question, "What does it seem to you?"—as does Matthew's version of the parable of the lost sheep (Matt. 18:12).[5] These questions are rather like ones that Jesus addresses to his audience in Luke in that they are questions at the beginning of parables. But they also both differ in their wording from the examples in Luke and cannot be readily explained as having been copied from Luke. A simple explanation accounts for these questions in both Matthew and Luke, namely, that Jesus regularly asked such questions before telling parables to engage his audience.

Common Endings to Parables

In Luke the story of the lost sheep ends as follows:

> I say to you that *thus* [Gk. *houtōs*, οὕτως] there will be joy in heaven over one sinner who repents rather than over ninety-nine righteous who do not have need of repentance. (Luke 15:7)

---

way to derive either the precise wording of Matt. 7:9–10 from Luke 11:11–12 or vice versa.

5 The same phrase is also used in Matt. 26:66 on the lips of the high priest at Jesus's trial, and the singular "What does it seem to you?" (Gk. *ti soi dokei*, τί σοι δοκεῖ) occurs in Matt. 17:25; 22:17.

CHAPTER 4

The parallel parable in Matthew ends in this way:

> *Thus* [Gk. *houtōs*, οὕτως] it is not the will of your Father in heaven that one of these little ones should perish. (Matt. 18:14)

These are not two versions of the same ending but two different but linguistically related ways of ending the same story, both beginning "thus." Since this feature of using "thus" to end a story is in both Matthew and Luke, it is likely that its use precedes the writing of both Gospels.[6] The parallel here is not so much in the wording of the story itself but in the *method* of storytelling. It points to a single storyteller whose words are recorded in both Gospels.

A second example of the same phenomenon in Luke 15 is found in the use of "it was necessary" (Gk. *edei*, ἔδει) in the closing speech of the authority figure in addressing someone who has failed to show compassion to his fellow:[7]

> But it was necessary [Gk. *edei*, ἔδει] to celebrate and be glad, for this your brother was dead and is alive again, and he was lost and is found. (Luke 15:32)

This parallels a statement at the end of a parable in Matthew that is structurally very similar to Luke 15; it too has a forgiv-

---

6 Harvey K. McArthur and Robert M. Johnston note the presence of "thus" in other parables of Jesus: Matt. 12:45; 13:49; 18:14, 35; 20:16; Mark 13:29; Luke 12:21; 14:33; 15:10; 17:10. *They Also Taught in Parables: Rabbinic Parables from the First Centuries of the Christian Era* (Grand Rapids, MI: Zondervan, 1990), 168–69.

7 Klyne R. Snodgrass, *Stories with Intent: A Comprehensive Guide to the Parables of Jesus*, 2nd ed. (Grand Rapids, MI: Eerdmans, 2018), 123.

ing authority figure with two subordinates and one refusing to forgive the other:

> Was it not necessary [Gk. *edei*, ἔδει] that you too should have had mercy on your fellow slave as I too had mercy on you? (Matt. 18:33)

Male and Female Pairs

The three stories of lost and found in Luke 15 have a unity between them. At the same time, two of these three stories have parallels in Matthew: the story of the lost sheep has a close parallel (Matt. 18:12–14), and the story of the two sons has a more distant one (Matt. 21:28–32). The story of the lost coin has no parallel in Matthew.

The stories of the lost sheep and the lost coin also have close parallels with each other and fit the pattern, often attributed to Luke, of male characters and female characters as the protagonists in adjacent texts.[8] Pairing male and female characters, however, is not something unique to Luke but is also found in Matthew and thus seems to go back to Jesus.[9] Consider the following examples:

---

8   Luke Timothy Johnson rightly claims, "It is typical of Luke to match a male example with one involving a woman (cf. 1:6–7; 2:36–38; 4:25, 38; 7:11–15, 36–50; 8:1–3, 19–21, 43–56; 10:38–42; 11:27; 13:10–17)." *The Gospel of Luke*, Sacra Pagina 3 (Collegeville, MN: Liturgical Press, 1991), 236. But merely appealing to Luke's activity does not provide adequate evidence that the pairs all result from Luke's compositional technique. Many of the instances listed are not pairs or are naturally occurring pairs. In some cases, such as Simeon and Anna (Luke 2:25–38), the pairing is presented as a part of a particular historical situation.

9   Kenneth E. Bailey, *Jacob and the Prodigal: How Jesus Retold Israel's Story* (Downers Grove, IL: InterVarsity Press, 2003), 89.

1. Matthew 12:41–42 (ESV; par. Luke 11:31–32)

    Male: The men of Nineveh will rise up at the judgment with this generation and condemn it, for they repented at the preaching of Jonah, and behold, something greater than Jonah is here.

    Female: The queen of the South will rise up at the judgment with this generation and condemn it, for she came from the ends of the earth to hear the wisdom of Solomon, and behold, something greater than Solomon is here.

2. Matthew 13:31–33 (ESV; par. Luke 13:18–21; partial par. Mark 4:30–32)

    Male: He put another parable before them, saying, "The kingdom of heaven is like a grain of mustard seed that a man took and sowed in his field. It is the smallest of all seeds, but when it has grown it is larger than all the garden plants and becomes a tree, so that the birds of the air come and make nests in its branches."

    Female: He told them another parable. "The kingdom of heaven is like leaven that a woman took and hid in three measures of flour, till it was all leavened."

3. Matthew 24:40–41 (ESV)

    Male: Then two men will be in the field; one will be taken and one left.

> Female: Two women will be grinding at the mill; one will
> be taken and one left.

The last example above has only a partial parallel in Luke, which features two men in a bed, rather than two men *in a field* (Luke 17:34–35 ESV):

> Male: I tell you, in that night there will be two in one
> bed. One will be taken and the other left.
> Female: There will be two women grinding together. One
> will be taken and the other left.

These final sayings in Matthew and Luke occur in similar contexts, but neither saying can easily be explained as a mere revision of the other. They can, however, readily be explained as varying examples by the same speaker, with the same *method* of communicating.

4. Matthew 25:1–30

A further pair in Matthew, in this case with the female example before the male, is the parable of the wise and foolish virgins (Matt. 25:1–13), which is followed by the parable of the talents, where large sums of money are assigned to male servants (Matt. 25:14–30). The most natural conclusion is that these pairings go back to Jesus.[10]

---

10 For a different set of arguments that gendered pairs go back to Jesus, see Sara Parks, *Gender in the Rhetoric of Jesus: Women in Q* (Lanham, MD: Lexington Books / Fortress Academic, 2019).

CHAPTER 4

Humans Worth More Than Sheep

The celebration in the story of the lost sheep in Luke 15:3–7 is similar to the celebration in the version of the story in Matthew 18:12–14, yet the wording is sufficiently different that it does not seem that one was directly copied from the other. Therefore, the attribution of a story of a lost sheep to Jesus seems to precede the Gospels of Matthew and Luke. Moreover, we have seen that Luke 15 has a climactic structure as we move from one hundred sheep to ten coins to two sons, with its finale in the story about lost humans. The logic of the structure is based on the fact that *a human is more valuable than a sheep*. It is just this logic that we find on Jesus's lips in Matthew's account of the healing of the man with the withered hand:

> He went on from there and entered their synagogue. And a man was there with a withered hand. And they asked him, "Is it lawful to heal on the Sabbath?"—so that they might accuse him. He said to them, "*Which one of you who has a sheep, if it falls into a pit on the Sabbath, will not take hold of it and lift it out? Of how much more value is a man than a sheep!* So it is lawful to do good on the Sabbath." Then he said to the man, "Stretch out your hand." And the man stretched it out, and it was restored, healthy like the other. (Matt. 12:9–13 ESV; cf. Mark 3:1–5; Luke 6:6–10)

The highlighted words in Matthew closely parallel the address in Luke 15:4 (ESV):

> "What man of you, having a hundred sheep, if . . . does not . . . ?"

In Matthew's version, Jesus asks a question about a sheep and then notes that a human is much more valuable than a sheep. The logic is the same as that of the entire chapter of Luke 15. The variation in wording between the three Gospels as they record the healing of the man with the withered hand prevents us from seeing the wording in Matthew as derived from Luke. Thus Matthew 12:10–12 and Luke 15:4–31 independently have a question at the beginning of an argument from the lesser to the greater about the relative value of sheep and humans. This pattern is simply explained if both go back to Jesus.

How to Address a Father

Matthew 21:28–32 has its own story of a father with two contrasting sons, one of whom initially responds badly and later does the right thing, and the other who initially responds positively but later does not do the right thing. The story is explicitly said to be in response to an approach by chief priests and elders (Matt. 21:23). The parable displays a similar storytelling mindset to that behind Luke 15:11–32, but again, it is hard to say that one could come from the other. The stories in their context are both applicable to similar audiences.

They also share the tiny feature of caring *how the son addresses his father*. In Luke 15:11–32 we saw that the younger son addresses his father as "Father," while the older son does not. In Matthew 21:28–32 the son who initially seems to reply well calls his father "sir," while the other offers an abrupt refusal. It is not that the two characters with polite addresses align. In fact, these parables connect the polite address with the characters who do not align between the parables, rather than with the ones who do. But each parable shows *the same skill* applied to the detail of how a character in a story might address an authority figure. This is naturally explained if the two stories go back to the same mind.

Stories Back-to-Back

Luke 15–16 contains a series of five stories told back-to-back, with the small interlude of Luke 16:10–18 between the final two stories. It presents a picture of Jesus as telling multiple stories back-to-back. This is, of course, something we see in Mark 4 and its parallels in Matthew 13 and to a lesser extent in Luke 8:4–18. It is also what happens with the three parables of Matthew 25. This sort of common feature is hard to explain as the result of one Gospel copying another since it would require analysis and imitation of the style of the preceding Gospel with no obvious benefit to doing so. Again, the most natural explanation is that telling stories or parables back-to-back is a pattern that comes from Jesus.

How Did Jesus's Stories Get Passed On?

It seems, then, that a common mind is behind the stories of Luke 15–16, and multiple lines of evidence suggest that the same mind is behind many other sayings attributed to Jesus. The storyteller of Luke 15–16 must be a gifted communicator, thoroughly familiar with the Old Testament and with the thought world of Jews in Palestine. The simplest hypothesis by far is that the storyteller is Jesus.

This does not explain *how* the stories were passed from Jesus into the Gospels, but that question, though tending to get primacy in academic discussion, is actually secondary. We may know that we have received a letter from a particular source without knowing the route the letter took to get to us, interesting though that may be. We may unexpectedly bump into a friend on vacation, but recognizing her does not depend on knowing how she got there. Similarly, we can recognize that the various stories discussed in this book show stylistic traits of an identifiable teacher without knowing how the stories were transmitted. We can acknowledge that a particular short story shows both internal coherence and the hallmarks of Jesus's teaching style without committing to a single theory of how the story was conveyed from Jesus's mouth to Luke's Gospel. To recognize Jesus's genius in the story of the two sons, we do not have to decide whether Jesus taught in Aramaic, Greek, or Hebrew—or in more than one of these languages. Nor do we need to decide how early Jesus's teachings were recorded in writing. These are all questions that I personally find fascinating but that are not necessary for recognizing the genius itself.

To put it another way, taking Jesus to be the author of the story of the two sons explains the brilliance of the story and the patterns we see across the Gospels. To reject the idea that Jesus is the genius behind the story merely because one cannot imagine how a two-and-a-half-minute story might have been reliably transmitted from Jesus to Luke's Gospel displays a distinct lack of imagination.

One way a story like this can be passed on is through repetition. We can observe that all four Gospels present Jesus as a teacher who repeated his teaching. They present him as saying identical or similar things on multiple occasions.

In Matthew, Jesus repeats sayings about divorce (5:32; 19:9); offending eyes (5:29; 18:9); offending hands (5:30; 18:8); trees known from their fruit (7:18–20; 12:33); desiring mercy and not sacrifice (9:13; 12:7); his followers being hated (10:22; 24:9); the lost sheep of the house of Israel (10:6; 15:24); wicked generations seeking signs (12:39; 16:4); the binding and loosing of things on earth and in heaven (16:19; 18:18); telling mountains to move (17:20; 21:21); the first being last (19:30; 20:16); those who are great needing to be servants (20:26; 23:11); many being deceived (24:5, 11); a place of weeping and gnashing of teeth (8:12; 13:42, 50; 22:13; 24:51; 25:30); those who already have being given more (13:12; 25:29); and those who have ears needing to hear (11:15; 13:9, 43). Jesus also predicts his passion three times (16:21; 17:22–23; 20:18–19).

In Mark, even though it contains significantly less speech by Jesus than the other Gospels, Jesus repeats sayings: those wanting to be first needing to be servants of all (9:35; 10:44); people not hearing (4:12; 8:18); "He who has ears to hear, let him hear" (4:9, 23); and, as in Matthew, the passion predictions (8:31; 9:31; 10:33–34).

In Luke, Jesus repeats things such as "Your faith has saved you / made you well" (7:50; 8:48; 17:19; 18:42); the command to show oneself to one or more priests (5:14; 17:14); "No one lights a lamp . . ." (8:16; 11:33); Pharisees/scribes "love the first seats" (11:43; 20:46); "Do not worry what you will say" (12:11–12; 21:14–15); "He who has ears to hear, let him hear" (8:8; 14:35); "Everyone who has, more will be given" (8:18; 19:26); and the passion predictions (9:22, 43b–44; 18:31–33).

In John, Jesus uses the words "Truly, truly I say to you" twenty-five times, and on six occasions he says, "I am going to the Father" (14:12, 28; 16:10, 17, 28; 20:17). Discourses regularly present variations on similar sayings. There are even repetitions of most of the "I am" sayings: "I am the bread of life" (6:48, 51); "I am the light of the world" (8:12; 9:5); "I am the door" (10:7, 9); "I am the good shepherd" (10:11, 14); "I am the resurrection and the life" (11:25) alongside "I am the way, the truth, and the life" (14:6); and "I am the true vine" (15:1) alongside "I am the vine" (15:5).

Thus, all four Gospels present us with a teacher who, like just about every other teacher in history, said the same things multiple times. Why think up an epigram like "Judge not, that you be not judged" (Matt. 7:1 ESV; cf. Luke 6:37), a saying like the Golden Rule (Matt. 7:12; Luke 6:31), or a story as captivating as Luke 15:11–32, and use it only once? If Jesus regularly repeated his teaching, then his disciples would have heard his stories numerous times, which makes it much easier to imagine how these stories could have been well preserved in the Gospels. Ultimately, we do not need to resolve the probably unanswerable question of how Jesus's teachings were transmitted early on in order to recognize that the stories attributed to him in the Gospels show numerous common features and that they are not readily explained as creations by the Gospel writers but are easily explained as the records of a brilliant teacher with a profile that closely matches what we know about Jesus.

Much More Than a Storyteller

WE HAVE SEEN converging lines of argument that Jesus is indeed the genius behind Luke 15 as well as behind other parables in the Gospels. We have also seen that Jesus knew and loved the Old Testament, which is a reminder to any who claim to follow him that they need to take the Old Testament seriously.

But it is not just that Jesus's longest story has an uncanny unity with the Old Testament; so also do the known facts of his life. We know from both Christian sources and the Roman historian Tacitus (ca. AD 56–ca. 120) when and by whom Jesus was executed. As Tacitus says,

Christ had undergone the death penalty during the reign of Tiberius, by sentence of the procurator Pontius Pilate.[1]

---

1 The Latin reads, *Christus Tiberio imperitante per procuratorem Pontium Pilatum supplicio adfectus erat*. Tacitus, *Annals* 15.44. Tacitus uses the later title procurator for Pilate when he was, in fact, a prefect.

Jesus died on a cross, a form of tree (Acts 5:30; 10:39; 13:29; Gal. 3:13; 1 Pet. 2:24), thereby bringing life. His death on a tree provides an answer to the question posed by the opening narrative of the Jewish Scriptures—the fateful scene at a tree when the first humans ate the forbidden fruit, came under a sentence of death, and were thrust out from paradise (Gen. 3). This story of death and exile from God's presence naturally raises the question of how relationship with God can be regained and whether there is any answer to death.

Quite independent from Christian records, a major Jewish source confirms the time of the year of Jesus's death:

On the eve of Passover, they hanged Jesus.[2]

Jesus was executed on the eve of the great annual Passover festival of the Jews, when they celebrated their exodus from slavery in Egypt. He died in the Jewish capital at the most significant festival in the Jewish calendar, just when that uniquely influential nation was shedding the blood of the largest number of animals and thinking of how the blood was shed on their behalf. They got together in households and sacrificed a Passover lamb and marked the doors of their houses with its blood, remembering what the ancient Israelites had done in Egypt. The Passover lamb symbolized a substitute. It died so that they did not need to. Are the timing, location, and method of Jesus's death just a coincidence?

---

2 The Hebrew is *Be'erev hapesakh tela'uhu leyeshu,* בערב הפסח תלאוהו לישו (Babylonian Talmud Sanhedrin 43a). The Babylonian Talmud is one of the most important collections of Jewish traditions, and though only completed about half a millennium after Jesus, it contains many traditions from the time of Jesus.

The four Gospels report that after his crucifixion, Jesus rose again and came back to life on the third day. The tomb was empty. There are many reports of people seeing him, including these words from the apostle Paul, written about AD 54:

> Then he appeared to more than five hundred brothers at one time, most of whom are still alive, though some have fallen asleep. (1 Cor. 15:6 ESV)

Numerous books have laid out the historical evidence for the resurrection of Jesus from the dead.[3] Still, thinking people today have often been rightly wary of the way some explain phenomena in the world with appeals to the supernatural. Such explanations are often seen as in tension with the methods of science, which brings us many advances in knowledge, whether in engineering, medicine, or physics. This is where the Christian claim that Jesus rose from the dead needs to be properly appreciated. It is not a claim for an anomaly within a universe otherwise guided by science. Rather, Jesus's resurrection *forms part of a pattern, not an anomaly*. It is one of a large number of remarkable things recorded about the person of Jesus.[4]

In this book we have examined Jesus's impressive storytelling ability but have not considered in detail any of the other striking things about him. We have not even examined his other forms

---

3 Two of many such defenses are the more popular William Lane Craig, *The Son Rises: The Historical Evidence for the Resurrection of Jesus* (Chicago: Moody Press, 1981), and the more technical N. T. Wright, *The Resurrection of the Son of God* (London: SPCK, 2003).

4 For some examples of this, see my book *Can We Trust the Gospels?* (Wheaton, IL: Crossway, 2018), 129–40.

of teaching. But from focusing on just one short story, we have seen his intimate knowledge of Genesis—a book historically documented to have been completed and accepted as Jewish Scripture centuries before he was born. Arguably, the connections of the story of the two sons with Genesis are so frequent that a literary critic who did not know the order in which things were written might more easily explain Genesis as an expansion of Luke 15 than explain Luke 15 as being based on Genesis. After all, it takes less skill to expand on the details of a story than to create a short story so simple yet thick with ideas drawn from a longer collection of stories. But once we accept that Jesus is more than simply a particularly brilliant human, we are free to see that the coordination of Genesis and Luke 15 can arise from God's own plan to shape the Genesis narrative with the purpose, among other things, of preparing for Jesus's longest story.

The beginning of the Jewish Bible, together with the finale offered by Jesus's life, death, and resurrection recorded in the New Testament, tell the greater story of a Creator God, whose commands we humans have disobeyed, making us subject to the death penalty. To have that penalty lifted, we need a substitute more valuable than a Passover lamb to take our place.

What if the great storyteller also lived a perfect life? What if he came from God? What if he was the long-anticipated Jewish Messiah? What if he was God's Son? All these things are claimed of Jesus in the Gospels, the very books that we have seen reliably reporting Jesus's words. If Jesus came from God, it would also explain how he could be such a genius.

The single best explanation for Jesus's genius is found at the beginning of John's Gospel, where the Word, later identified as

Jesus Christ (John 1:14, 17), is described both as alongside God and as God himself:

> In the beginning was the Word, and the Word was with God, and the Word was God. (John 1:1)

If the storyteller Jesus Christ is God himself, who made the world, invented language, oversaw history, and then became human to tell us about God and to rescue us from our alienation to him, then his wisdom and genius make sense. And if he is that smart and if he also loved us enough to die to save us, the only sensible thing to do is to accept him unreservedly as our teacher, guide, and Savior.

General Index

Scripture Index

Ancient Sources Index

Also Available from
Peter J. Williams

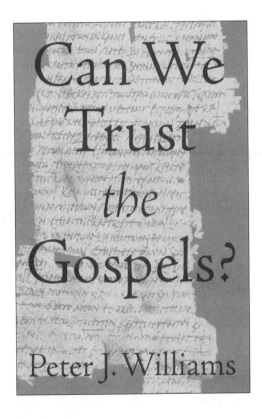

Written for the skeptic and the believer, the uninitiated and the scholar, this introduction to the historical and theological reliability of the four Gospels helps readers better understand the arguments in favor of trusting them.

For more information, visit **crossway.org**.